Welcome to Reiki 1

Index:

Introduction to Reiki:
History Of Reiki
Reiki, Universal Life Force
How Reiki Works
Five Reiki Principals
Preparing for Reiki 1
Anatomy For Reiki 1
Reiki Self Treatment
Preparing to Treat Others
Treating Others
Rapid Reiki Treatment
Pregnancy, Babies and Children
Using Your Imagination
Final Thought

About This Course

Introduction to Reiki I is a training guide to help you understand and put into practice what you know and learn about Usui Reiki. It is an in-depth course and will help you on your journey to becoming a professional Reiki Practitioner.

Practice at home on friends and family and let them experience Reiki healing. Once you have practiced and filled in the log sheet attached to this manual, submit this and the small examination to info@mysticspirit.co.za and upon successful completion, you will receive your certificate and Reiki I Attunement.

It is advised that before commencing with Reiki I, you purchase Astara's Ultimate Chakra Guide as this goes in depth on all the different Chakras, their corresponding organs and how to see when they are unbalanced. This will give you a thorough understanding and it will make Reiki I easier when it comes to hand placements and types of treatments. This will further be beneficial when you do my Reiki for Animals course, as it focuses on the different Chakras.

Enjoy the course and feel free to submit any questions to info@mysticspirit.co.za. I look forward to taking you on this journey of healing and growth.

Mystic Spirit

Section One

Introduction To Reiki

Reiki, pronounced Ray-Key, can be translated to mean universal life force. It is the gift of vitality and self-preservation encoded into the genetic makeup of all living things.

It is believed that Reiki has been practiced for thousands of years and was rediscovered by Dr. Mikao Usui, in the 19th century. Dr. Usui, born in Japan, discovered the power of healing while researching ancient Buddhist documents. After discovering these revelations, he went on to share them with others, who then passed it on from Masters to Students throughout the centuries and made its way to the West in the 1960s and 1970's..

The most common misconception is that the Reiki practitioner is your healer when in reality, it is your client who is opening their heart to healing themselves. You as a practitioner are merely the conduit for energy to pass through. It is, therefore, very important that you and your client both understand this before starting a healing session. That way, there will be no unrealistic expectations for either of you.

Lesson 1: The History of Reiki

The Japanese like many ancient cultures used word of mouth to pass their history and practices down from generation to generation. Unfortunately, this led to a great deal of knowledge and wisdom being watered down and lost. Many people involved with Reiki believe that the techniques we use today for healing were first used in India by Buddha and later by Jesus.

The following referenced history of Reiki is taken from Reiki, The Healing Touch, by William Lee Rand and has been carefully researched to contain verified information from dependable sources. There have been many attempts to explain the history of Reiki, but unfortunately, in the past, many of them have been based more on myth and an attempt to validate a particular style of Reiki and for the most part, lacked accurate information. Realizing the need for a factually based history of Reiki, I've spent over twenty years researching this information based on written records and interviews with those close to its development. The result is the following history of Reiki, which is derived from evidence-based facts.
Mikao Usui, or Usui Sensei as he is called by Reiki students in Japan, was born August 15, 1865, in the village of Taniai in the Yamagata district of Gifu prefecture, which is located near present-day Nagoya, Japan. (4)
He had an avid interest in learning and worked hard at his studies. As he grew older, he traveled to Europe and China to further his education. His curriculum included medicine, psychology, and religion as well as the art of divination, which Asians have long considered to be a worthy skill. (5) Usui Sensei also became a member of the Rei Jyutu Ka, a metaphysical group dedicated to developing psychic abilities. (6) He had many jobs including civil servant, company employee, and journalist, and he helped rehabilitate prisoners. (7) Eventually he became the secretary to Shinpei Goto, head of the department of health and welfare who later became the mayor of Tokyo. The connections Usui Sensei made at this job helped him to also become a successful businessman.

The depth and breadth of his experiences inspired him to direct his attention toward discovering the purpose of life. In his search he came across the description of a special state of consciousness that once achieved would not only provide an understanding of one's life purpose but would also guide one to achieve it. This special state is called An-shin Ritus-mei (pronounced on sheen dit sue may). In this special state, one is always at peace regardless of what is taking place in the outer world. And it is from this place of peace that one completes one's life purpose. One of the special features of this state is that it maintains itself without any effort on the part of the individual; the experience of peace simply wells up spontaneously from within and is a type of enlightenment.

Usui Sensei understood this concept on an intellectual level and dedicated his life to achieving it; this is considered to be an important step on Usui Sensei's spiritual path. He discovered that one path to An-shin Ritsu-mei is through the practice of Zazen meditation. So he found a Zen teacher who accepted him as a student and began to practice Zazen. After three years of practice, he had not been successful and sought further guidance. His teacher suggested a more severe practice in which the student must be willing to die to achieve An-shin Ritsu-mei. (9, 10)

So with this in mind, he prepared for death and in February 1922, he went to Kurama Yama, a sacred mountain north of Kyoto. He went to fast and meditate until he passed to the next world. It must kept in mind that he was not looking to discover a method of healing, but was seeking to experience this special spiritual state. In addition, we know there is a small waterfall on Kurama Yama where even today people go to meditate. This meditation involves standing under the waterfall and allowing the water to strike and flow over the top of the head, a practice that is said to activate the crown chakra. Japanese Reiki Masters think that Usui Sensei may have used this meditation as part of his

practice. In any case, as time passed he became weaker and weaker. It was now March 1922 and at midnight of the twenty-first day, a powerful light suddenly entered his mind through the top of his headand he felt as if he had been struck by lightning; this caused him to fall unconscious

Tenyo Shrine is a short walk from where Usui Sensei was born in the village of Taniai. The Torii or archway is inscribed with words indicating that it was donated by Usui Mikao in 1923.
As the sun rose, he awoke and realized that whereas before he had felt very weak and near death from his fasting, he was now filled with an extremely enjoyable state of vitality that he had never experienced before; a miraculous type of high-frequency spiritual energy had displaced his normal consciousness and replaced it with an amazing new level of awareness. He experienced himself as being the energy and consciousness of the Universe and that the special state of enlightenment he had sought had been given

When this happened, he was filled with excitement and went running down the mountain to tell his Zen master of his great good fortune. On his way down he stubbed his toe on a rock and fell. And as anyone would do, he placed his hands over the toe, which was in pain. As he did this, healing energy began flowing from his hands all by itself. The pain in his toe went away and the toe was healed. Usui Sensei was amazed by this. He realized that in addition to the illuminating experience he had undergone, he had also received the gift of healing. He also understood that this was his

In April 1922, he moved to Tokyo and started a healing society that he named Usui Reiki Ryoho Gakkai (Usui Reiki Healing Method Society). He also opened a Reiki clinic in Harajuku, Aoyama, Tokyo. There he taught classes and gave treatments. (12)
At first, all Usui Sensei had was the healing energy. Over time he developed his system of Reiki practice. Most of these developments came in 1923 after the Great Kanto earthquake and tsunami that did extensive damage in Tokyo and killed and injured many thousands of people. Because there were so many people in need of healing, Usui Sensei decided he needed to do something to

It was at this time that he developed many of his practitioner techniques such as Gassho, Byosen scanning, Reiji-ho, Gyoshi ho, Seishin-to-itsu, and so forth. He also developed a formal attunement method or Reiju kai, making it easier for others to learn Reiki and to become teachers. Before this, the method he used to pass on the Reiki ability was to simply hold the students' hands, but this took a long time. The Reiju kai made transferring the Reiki ability much faster. Also, he had many different ways he performed the Reiju Kai, not just one. (13) During this time he also developed the Reiki symbols of which he had only three. These are the three symbols that we currently receive in Reiki II, which he called Okuden. He did not have a Master symbol. This important point was confirmed by Hiroshi Doi Sensei, a member of the Gakkai, and in discussions, he had with several of the Gakkai presidents and many of the Shinpiden members. (14) This idea was also confirmed by Arjava Petter Sensei, who had contact with Shinpiden teachers from the Gakkai and with its president. (15)

These same sources also indicate that Usui Sensei also gave many attunements to each student, not just one or one set. The purpose of the student receiving the attunement over and over was that this process continually acted to refine and develop one's ability to channel Reiki energy, thus making the energy one channeled more versatile and able to heal a wider range of conditions, to heal more deeply and in a shorter time. The philosophy of Usui Sensei was that there is no limit to the quality and effectiveness of the Reiki energy available in the universe and an important purpose for all students was to continually seek to improve the quality and effectiveness of the Reiki energy one can channel. (16)

He called his system of healing Shin-Shin Kai-Zen Usui Reiki Ryo-Ho (The Usui Reiki Treatment Method for Improvement of Body and Mind)(17) or in its simplified form Usui Reiki Ryoho (Usui Reiki Healing Method).

The first degree of his training was called Shoden (First Degree) and was divided into four levels: Loku-Tou, Go-Tou, Yon-Tou, and San-Tou. (Note that when Takata Sensei taught this level, which in the West we refer to as Reiki Level I, she combined all four levels into one. This is most likely why she did four attunements for Level I.) The next degree was called Okuden (Inner Teaching) and had two levels: Okuden-Zen-ki (first part), and Okuden-Koe-ki (second part). The next degree was called Shinpiden (Mystery Teaching), which is what Western Reiki calls Master level. The Shinpiden level includes Shihan-Kaku (assistant teacher) and Shihan (venerable teacher). (18)

Demand for Reiki became so great that Usui Sensei outgrew his clinic, so in 1925 he built a bigger one in Nakano, Tokyo. Because of this, his reputation as a healer spread all over Japan. He began to travel so he could teach and treat more people. During his travels across Japan, he directly taught more than 2,000 students and initiated twenty Shihan,(19) each being given the same understanding of Reiki and approved to teach and give Reiju in the same way that he did. (20)

The Japanese government issued him a Kun San To award for doing honorable work to help others. (21) While traveling to Fukuyama to teach, he suffered a stroke and died on March 9, 1926. (22) His grave is at Saihoji Temple, in Suginami, Tokyo, although some claim that his ashes are located elsewhere. After Usui Sensei died, his students erected a memorial stone next to his gravestone. Mr. J. Ushida, a Shihan trained by Usui Sensei, took over as president of the Usui Reiki Ryoho Gakkai and was responsible for creating and erecting the Usui Memorial stone and ensuring that the gravesite would be maintained. Mr. Ushida was followed by Mr. Ilichi Taketomi, Mr. Yoshiharu Watanabe, Mr. Toyoichi Wanami and Ms. Kimiko Koyama. The current successor to Usui Sensei is Mr. Mahayoshi Kondo, who became

Contrary to what we have been told in the West, there is no "lineage bearer" or "Grand Master" of the organization started by Usui Sensei—only the succession of presidents listed above. (23) Among the twenty teachers initiated by Usui Sensei are Toshihiro Eguchi, Jusaburo Guida, Kan'ichi Taketomi, Toyoichi Wanami, Yoshiharu Watanabe, Keizo Ogawa, J. Ushida, and Chujiro Hayashi. (24) Contrary to one version of the Reiki story, Mr. J. Ushida, not Chujiro Hayashi, was the Gakkai's successor to Usui Sensei. It is also important to note that the first four presidents of the Gakkai who followed Usui Sensei were Shihan who had been trained directly by Usui Sensei, and the last of these was president of the Gakkai through 1975, thus assuring that the Gakkai understanding, practice and teaching methods were the same as that of Usui Sensei.

Tenyo Shrine is a short walk from where Usui Sensei was born in the village of Taniai. The Torii or archway is inscribed with words indicating that it was donated by Usui Mikao in 1923.

As the sun rose, he awoke and realized that whereas before he had felt very weak and near death from his fasting, he was now filled with an extremely enjoyable state of vitality that he had never experienced before; a miraculous type of high-frequency spiritual energy had displaced his normal consciousness and replaced it with an amazing new level of awareness. He experienced himself as being the energy and consciousness of the Universe and that the special state of enlightenment he had sought had been given to him as a gift. He was overjoyed by this realization.

When this happened, he was filled with excitement and went running down the mountain to tell his Zen master of his great good fortune. On his way down he stubbed his toe on a rock and fell. And as anyone would do, he placed his hands over the toe, which was in pain. As he did this, healing energy began flowing from his hands all by itself. The pain in his toe went away and the toe was healed. Usui Sensei was amazed by this. He realized that in addition to the illuminating experience he had undergone, he had also received the gift of healing. He also understood that this was his life purpose; to be a healer and to train others. (11)

In April 1922, he moved to Tokyo and started a healing society that he named Usui Reiki Ryoho Gakkai (Usui Reiki Healing Method Society). He also opened a Reiki clinic in Harajuku, Aoyama, Tokyo. There he taught classes and gave treatments. (12)

At first, all Usui Sensei had was the healing energy. Over time he developed his system of Reiki practice. Most of these developments came in 1923 after the Great Kanto earthquake and tsunami that did extensive damage in Tokyo and killed and injured many thousands of people. Because there were so many people in need of healing, Usui Sensei decided he needed to do something to speed up his ability to train teachers

It was at this time that he developed many of his practitioner techniques such as Gassho, Byosen scanning, Reiji-ho, Gyoshi ho, Seishin-to-itsu, and so forth. He also developed a formal attunement method or Reiju kai, making it easier for others to learn Reiki and to become teachers. Before this, the method he used to pass on the Reiki ability was to simply hold the students' hands, but this took a long time. The Reiju kai made transferring the Reiki ability much faster. Also, he had many different ways he performed the Reiju Kai, not just one. (13) During this time he also developed the Reiki symbols of which he had only three. These are the three symbols that we currently receive in Reiki II, which he called Okuden. He did not have a Master symbol. This important point was confirmed by Hiroshi Doi Sensei, a member of the Gakkai, and in discussions, he had with several of the Gakkai presidents and many of the Shinpiden members. (14) This idea was also confirmed by Arjava Petter Sensei, who had contact with Shinpiden teachers from the Gakkai and with its president. (15)

These same sources also indicate that Usui Sensei also gave many attunements to each student, not just one or one set. The purpose of the student receiving the attunement over and over was that this process continually acted to refine and develop one's ability to channel Reiki energy, thus making the energy one channeled more versatile and able to heal a wider range of conditions, to heal more deeply and in a shorter time. The philosophy of Usui Sensei was that there is no limit to the quality and effectiveness of the Reiki energy available in the universe and an important purpose for all students was to continually seek to improve the quality and effectiveness of the Reiki energy one can channel. (16)

He called his system of healing Shin-Shin Kai-Zen Usui Reiki Ryo-Ho (The Usui Reiki Treatment Method for Improvement of Body and Mind)(17) or in its simplified form Usui Reiki Ryoho (Usui Reiki Healing Method).

The first degree of his training was called Shoden (First Degree) and was divided into four levels: Loku-Tou, Go-Tou, Yon-Tou, and San-Tou. (Note that when Takata Sensei taught this level, which in the West we refer to as Reiki Level I, she combined all four levels into one. This is most likely why she did four attunements for Level I.) The next degree was called Okuden (Inner Teaching) and had two levels: Okuden-Zen-ki (first part), and Okuden-Koe-ki (second part). The next degree was called Shinpiden (Mystery Teaching), which is what Western Reiki calls Master level. The Shinpiden level includes Shihan-Kaku (assistant teacher) and Shihan (venerable teacher). (18)

Demand for Reiki became so great that Usui Sensei outgrew his clinic, so in 1925 he built a bigger one in Nakano, Tokyo. Because of this, his reputation as a healer spread all over Japan. He began to travel so he could teach and treat more people. During his travels across Japan, he directly taught more than 2,000 students and initiated twenty Shihan,(19) each being given the same understanding of Reiki and approved to teach and give Reiju in the same way that he did. (20)

The Japanese government issued him a Kun San To award for doing honorable work to help others. (21) While traveling to Fukuyama to teach, he suffered a stroke and died on March 9, 1926. (22) His grave is at Saihoji Temple, in Suginami, Tokyo, although some claim that his ashes are located elsewhere.

After Usui Sensei died, his students erected a memorial stone next to his gravestone. Mr. J. Ushida, a Shihan trained by Usui Sensei, took over as president of the Usui Reiki Ryoho Gakkai and was responsible for creating and erecting the Usui Memorial stone and ensuring that the gravesite would be maintained. Mr. Ushida was followed by Mr. Ilichi Taketomi, Mr. Yoshiharu Watanabe, Mr. Toyoichi Wanami and Ms. Kimiko Koyama. The current successor to Usui Sensei is Mr. Mahayoshi Kondo, who became president in 1998.

Contrary to what we have been told in the West, there is no "lineage bearer" or "Grand Master" of the organization started by Usui Sensei—only the succession of presidents listed above. (23) Among the twenty teachers initiated by Usui Sensei are Toshihiro Eguchi, Jusaburo Guida, Kan'ichi Taketomi, Toyoichi Wanami, Yoshiharu Watanabe, Keizo Ogawa, J. Ushida, and Chujiro Hayashi. (24) Contrary to one version of the Reiki story, Mr. J. Ushida, not Chujiro Hayashi, was the Gakkai's successor to Usui Sensei. It is also important to note that the first four presidents of the Gakkai who followed Usui Sensei were Shihan who had been trained directly by Usui Sensei, and the last of these was president of the Gakkai through 1975, thus assuring that the Gakkai understanding, practice and teaching methods were the same as that of Usui Sensei

Dr Mikao Usui
Founder & 1st Grand Master

Chujiro Hayashi

Before his passing, Usui Sensei had asked Chujiro Hayashi Sensei to open his own Reiki clinic and to expand and develop Reiki Ryoho based on his previous experience as a medical doctor in the Navy. Motivated by this request, Hayashi Sensei started a school and clinic called Hayashi Reiki Kenkyukai (Institute). After Usui Sensei's passing, he left the Gakkai. (25)

At his clinic, which was located in Tokyo, he kept careful records of all the illnesses and conditions of his Reiki patients. He also kept records of which Reiki hand positions worked best to treat each illness and condition. Based on these records he created the Reiki Ryoho Shinshin (Guidelines for Reiki Healing Method). (26) This healing guide was part of a class manual he gave to his students. The handbook was to be used only if the practitioner was not able to use Byosen scanning to find the best hand positions to use. Many of his students received their Reiki training in return for working in his clinic. (27)

Hayashi Sensei also changed the way Reiki sessions were given. Rather than have the client seated in a chair and treated by one practitioner as Usui Sensei had done, Hayashi Sensei had the client lie on a treatment table and receive treatment from several practitioners at a time. He also created a new, more effective system for giving Reiju (attunements). (28) In addition, to increase the value his students received while he was traveling, he developed a new method of teaching Reiki. In this method, he taught both Shoden and Okuden (Reiki I&II) together in one five-day seminar. Each day included two to three hours of instruction and one Reiju. (29) Following the Usui method, students were encouraged to receive Reiju regularly from their local Shihan or teacher after completing Hayashi Sensei's class to continue to refine and develop the quality of the Reiki energy that they channeled.

Current photo of where Hayashi Sensei's Reiki clinic was located in Toyko.

Because of his trip to Hawaii in 1937–38 before the Japanese attack on Pearl Harbor, he was asked by the Japanese military to provide information about the location of warehouses and other military targets in Honolulu. He refused to do so and was declared a traitor. This caused him to "lose face," which meant he and his family would be disgraced and would be ostracized from Japanese society. The only solution was seppuku (ritual suicide), which he carried out. He died honorably on May 11, 1940. (30)

After this, Hayashi Sensei's wife Chie Hayashi took over his clinic and ran it for some years, but eventually, she retired; with no one to take over this position, the clinic came to an end. Some of Hayashi Sensei's students likely continued to teach but most of these have also passed on. In 1999 it was discovered that Chiyoko Yamaguchi Sensei, a Shinpiden or Master student of Hayashi Sensei, was still alive and practicing. She was encouraged to teach and began doing so. Fortunately, I was able to take her Reiki I&II class in 2001 in Kyoto, Japan. Chiyoko Yamaguchi passed on in 2003.

Hawayo Takata

The following is a summary of Takata Sensei's version of her early years leading up to her contact with Reiki at the Hayashi clinic. It comes from an interview that appeared in The (San Mateo) Times, May 17, 1975, titled "Mrs. Takata Opens Minds to Reiki" by Vera Graham:

She stated that she was born on December 24th, 1900, on the island of Kauai, Hawaii. Her parents were Japanese immigrants and her father worked in the sugar cane fields. She eventually married the bookkeeper of the plantation where she was employed. His name was Saichi Takata and they had two daughters. In October 1930, Saichi died at the age of 34, leaving Mrs. Takata to raise their two children.

To provide for her family, she had to work very hard with little rest. After five years she developed severe abdominal pain and a lung condition, and she had a nervous breakdown. Soon after this one of her sisters died and it was Takata Sensei's responsibility to travel to Japan, where her parents had resettled to deliver the news. She also felt she could receive help for her health issues in Japan. After informing her parents and attending the funeral, she entered a hospital and stated that she was diagnosed with a tumor, gallstones, appendicitis, and asthma. She was told to prepare for an operation but opted to visit Hayashi Sensei's clinic instead.

Mrs. Takata was unfamiliar with Reiki but was impressed that the diagnosis of Reiki practitioners at the clinic closely matched the doctors at the hospital. She began receiving treatments. Two Reiki practitioners would treat her each day. The heat from their hands was so strong, she said, that she thought they were secretly using some kind of equipment. Seeing the large sleeves of the Japanese kimono worn by one, she thought she had found the secret place of concealment. Grabbing his sleeves one day she startled the practitioner, but, of course, found nothing. When she explained what she was doing, he began to laugh and then told her about Reiki and how it worked

Mrs. Takata got progressively better and in four months was completely healed. She wanted to learn Reiki for herself. In the spring of 1936, she received First Degree Reiki from Dr. Hayashi. She then worked with him for a year and received Second Degree Reiki. Mrs. Takata returned to Hawaii in 1937, followed shortly thereafter by Hayashi Sensei, who came to help establish Reiki there, and his daughter. In February 1938, Hayashi Sensei initiated Hawayo Takata as a Reiki Master.

This house is where Takata Sensei's clinic was located in Hilo, Hawaii where she gave Reiki sessions from 1939 to 1949.

Takata Sensei practiced Reiki in Hawaii, establishing several clinics, one of which was located in Hilo on the Big Island. She gave treatments and initiated students up to Reiki II. She became a well known healer and traveled to the U.S. mainland and other parts of the world teaching and giving treatments. She was a powerful healer who attributed her success to the fact that she did a lot of Reiki on each client. She would often do multiple treatments, each sometimes lasting hours, and treat difficult cases every day for months until the client was healed. To help with this process, she often initiated members of a client's family so they could give Reiki to the client as well.

Takata Sensei had a unique way of practicing and teaching Reiki that was noticeably different than how Usui Sensei or Hayashi Sensei had practiced and taught. The late John Harvey Gray was one of Takata Sensei's most respected students and she indicated that he would be one of three Reiki Masters that were to carry on her work after she retired

31) He indicates in his Reiki book that Takata Sensei had changed the way she taught Reiki because she said that the Japanese style was too complicated and would be difficult for the Western mind to learn. Because of this, she said she had simplified the system. This included the development of her hand position system, which she called the foundation treatment. This consisted of eight hand positions, which were on the abdomen, the shoulders, and the head. She also included some additional positions for the back if the client needed them. (32) This varied considerably from how Usui Sensei and Hayashi Sensei practiced in that they taught Byosen scanning as the way to find the best hand positions for treatment. They also indicated that Byosen scanning was the most important practice technique for a student to master after the practice of continually receiving repeated Reijus. Yet, Takata Sensei never taught this technique. She also did not teach any of the other methods used by Usui Sensei and Hayashi Sensei such as Gassho, Reiji-ho, Kenyoku, Gyoshi-ho, Koki-ho, and so forth. Additionally, she had a different attunement method for each level of Reiki, taught her students that the attunements empowered the symbols, and taught a Master symbol that was given to Master students. In her system, the Master symbol was needed to give attunements, and it could also be used during Reiki sessions for purposes of healing. She did not encourage her students to receive as many attunements as possible as was taught by Usui Sensei and Hayashi Sensei but taught that just one set of four attunements for Reiki I and one or two attunements for Reiki II and one for the Master level are all that is necessary. (33)

The simplified system that Takata Sensei taught was effective and has proven to produce valuable results for her students and their clients. Because of this, Takata Sensei can be considered an important innovator of Usui Reiki Ryoho.

One thing that is important to understand is that if it were not for Takata Sensei, Reiki would most likely have fallen into obscurity and never have been practiced by people all over the world; even in Japan, it would have been mostly unknown. This is because, after World War II, the United States required Japan to unconditionally surrender. This placed the United States in complete control of Japan. One of the conditions the U.S. required is that all those practicing any kind of healing be required to have a license. Some of the healing groups did get licensed, but the Usui Reiki Ryoho Gakkai decided that they did not want to be controlled by a licensing board and instead chose to go underground. They decided that the members were not to talk to anyone outside their group about Reiki and that they would only practice Reiki with each other. This made it difficult for anyone to find out about Reiki in Japan including the Japanese. Also, because it became very difficult for new members to join, the membership slowly declined. This problem exists even now, and the Gakkai membership continues to slowly dwindle. If this continues, at some time in the not too distant future the Gakkai is likely to come to an end.

Because Takata Sensei learned Reiki in Japan and returned to Hawaii and began teaching Reiki before World War II, she prevented Reiki from being lost. She was a great teacher and promoter and taught Reiki classes all over Hawaii and in many parts of the U.S. mainland. Before her passing, she taught 22 Reiki Masters who carried on the tradition.

The Evolution of Reiki

One thing I came to realize from my training experience is that there is no limit to the possibilities offered by Reiki. As demonstrated by Usui Sensei, Hayashi Sensei, and Takata Sensei, Reiki is something that is meant to be developed. This is true for the techniques one uses to practice Reiki, but it is also true for the quality of the healing energy.
Reiki energy comes from an infinite source and because of this, regardless of how developed and evolved one's healing energy has become, one will always be channeling only a small portion of the potential healing energy that is available; it is always possible for the quality, effectiveness, and benefit of one's healing energies to improve and this includes what takes place in the Attunements, Placements, and Ignitions.
Usui Sensei alluded to this when he said he wasn't at the top of the Reiki healing system, but one step below. (34) It is also important to note that according to the Bible, Jesus, who is considered by many to be a great healer and spiritual master, said that we could do everything he had done and even more. (35)

Reiki Continues to Develop

Takata Sensei required all the Masters she trained to charge a fee of $10,000 for the Master level. She taught that this was a required fee, and if you did not charge this fee, then you would not be teaching Usui Reiki. The fee wasn't based on the length or quality of training she provided, as no apprenticeship was included. (36) The actual length of her Master's training has not been documented by any of her Masters, except for Bethel Phaigh, who reported receiving both Level II and Master within a few days. (37) However, my conversations with a few of her Masters indicate in at least some cases her Master training lasted only a few days. According to Phage, the high fee was to instill respect for the Master level. However, the high fee, along with the tendency of Takata Sensei's Masters not to teach many other Masters, was causing Reiki to spread very slowly.

Iris Ishikuro was one of Takata Sensei's Master students and Iris also had other training as a healer. She was involved with the Johrei Fellowship, a religious fellowship that includes healing with energy projected from the hands. (38) She had also learned another kind of healing from her sister, who worked in a Tibetan temple in Hawaii. After Takata Sensei passed in 1980, Iris decided that she would follow her inner guidance and teach for a more reasonable fee. As far as I know, she was the only one of Takata Sensei's twenty-two Masters who did this. The others continued to charge the high fee for Mastership.

Iris trained only two Masters. One was Arthur Robertson and the other was her daughter, Ruby. She asked them to always charge a reasonable fee. Ruby decided not to teach Reiki. However, Arthur Robertson did begin teaching in the mid-1980s. The reasonable fee allowed many more students to become Reiki Masters. He began giving Master training with ten to thirty students in each class. Those that Robertson taught trained others and the number of teaching Reiki Masters quickly increased.

Because Iris Ishikuro ignored the price restriction that Takata Sensei had placed on Reiki, she became the pathway through which Reiki would spread more quickly and eventually be passed on to people all over the world. In light of this, the majority of Reiki people in the world likely have their lineage going back through Iris Ishikuro.

Arthur Robertson had also been a teacher of Tibetan shamanism and had learned a healing method that made use of several symbols and an attunement-like technique called empowerment. This method had similarities to Usui Reiki. After becoming a Reiki Master, he developed an alternative method of Reiki that was a combination of the Tibetan style of healing and Usui Reiki. The parts from Tibetan shamanism were the use of two Tibetan symbols—with one being used as a Master symbol—and the Violet Breath. It also incorporated the use of the three symbols from the Okuden level of Usui Reiki. He called this system Raku Kei. (39)

The Essence of Reiki

As we meditate on Reiki energy, both when giving treatments to others and to ourselves and when teaching classes and giving attunements, and now with Holy Fire Reiki when giving Placements and Ignitions we become aware of a wealth of positive qualities that are embodied within the essence of the Reiki energy. These qualities transcend states of consciousness we usually are aware of and take us up into ever more refined feelings of peace, joy, and happiness. In addition, they are also capable of helping us develop healthy, positive traits in our personalities.

However, since Reiki respects free will, it will not heal us or develop these higher states unless we invite it to do so. This requires that we be willing to change. The ability to recognize unhealthy personal qualities within ourselves and be willing to let them go is necessary if we are to move forward with our healing. Those who accept Reiki as their spiritual path and are devoted to allowing it to heal them completely and surrender to its ability to do this find that Reiki will guide them more quickly along the path of healing. This process can include improving the quality of the Reiki energy that one can channel as well as helping to develop all the qualities that are healthy for a person to have.

As the quality improves, Reiki can heal us and those who come to us for Reiki sessions and classes more easily and more deeply. As the quality of Reiki energy one can channel becomes more refined and effective, one becomes more aware of the essence of Reiki and the amazing places it is capable of taking us.

The positive, healthy traits Reiki is capable of developing within us include patience, love of self and others, non-competitiveness. It moves us into a place of acceptance of others' ideas and beliefs and helps us to be non-judgmental, empowers our ability to forgive, develops gratitude for friends and family and for all we have and experience, improves the quality of joy and peace we experience and most importantly increases our connection to the Source of Reiki so that an ever-stronger feeling of safety develops as Reiki more easily guides our lives and watches over all that we do.

This understanding helps us to appreciate that Reiki has unlimited potential. This idea is validated by the fact that both Usui Sensei and Hayashi Sensei encouraged their students to further refine and improve the quality of Reiki they were able to channel. It is also apparent from the idea that if Reiki does come from an unlimited potential as most Reiki people agree, then no matter how effective our Reiki has become, it's always possible for it to become more effective. This concept can be likened to a library. Once one has a library card, one has access to the books in the library, but that doesn't mean that one has read all the books and can apply all the knowledge and wisdom they contain. The same is true of Reiki. Simply having received the attunements or Ignitions does give you access to the Reiki energy, but that doesn't mean you can channel the highest and most effective qualities of Reiki that exist. It simply means you now can access the Reiki energy and if you permit it and work with it, it can refine your ability to channel ever higher and more effective levels of healing energy. This awareness becomes even more apparent with Holy Fire Reiki and, as you shall experience in this class, an ever-higher level of joy, peace, and love will show you how wonderful and important it is to allow yourself to receive this gift.

Section Two

Lesson 2: Reiki the Universal Life Force

We know that every living thing on earth has an energy or life force and for thousands of years, we have tried to find ways to develop this force and improve and influence our lives. The Japanese called this energy Ki. Also known as Chi, by the Chinese. It has also been scientifically proven that this energy surrounds us. It is within and around us, and we can even see this energy with the help of Kirlian photography.
Many successful disciplines such as Reiki, Tai Chi, Feng Shui, Meditation, Yoga and Acupuncture have been developed to control and greatly increase the flow of this energy in and around the body

By practicing the discipline of Reiki, you regain your natural ability to heal yourself and others as well as the knowledge you need to lead a happier and more fulfilling life. By understanding and learning how to use this Reiki energy, you will enhance not only your own life but the lives of your clients as well. For this reason, it is very important to understand how Reiki works. With Reiki, we can do this by touching our customers or by holding your hands just above them.

The best part about Reiki is that it is free energy. The only thing you need as a practitioner is a discipline to learn and practice until you master your craft and enjoy this life-changing journey you are about to begin.

While I was studying massage therapy, it became very obvious that touch can be soothing and healing. For example: when you were a child and fell and scraped your knee, your mom would rub it and even kiss it better. The rubbing of the ouchie made you feel instantly better, even though the pain was still very much there. If you were not feeling well and your mom held you it comforted you and soothed you. Reiki works in the same way. The energy we allow to flow through us has the soothing and healing we received as children through touch. With Reiki, we can either perform it by touching our clients or by holding our hands just above them.

Lesson 3: What is Reiki?

Reiki is a form of manual healing, originating in India and the East, dating back thousands of years before the time of Christ and Buddha. The original name, disciplines, and techniques of Reiki have been lost due to the traditional method being passed down from generation to generation. It is difficult to pinpoint exactly when this ancient healing art disappeared. However, we do know that it was rediscovered by a Japanese scholar and monk named Dr. Mikao Usui. It was Dr. Usui who named REIKI.

Reiki is a two-syllable Japanese word meaning universal life force. Although the correct Japanese pronunciation is RYE-KEY, it has been westernized to RAY-KEY.

Rei means universal. Esoterically, Rei means spiritual consciousness, omniscient wisdom from God, or the higher self.
Ki is the non-physical vitality that gives life to all living things. Many cultures understand and accept the importance of Ki energy and how it affects our lives and well-being.

霊

Rei - Universal

気

Ki - Life Force

Ki energy can be activated for healing purposes. When you feel healthy and enthusiastic, the flow of Ki energy in your body is high. It seems easier to deal with life and you have a higher resistance to illness and disease.

However, when your Ki energy is low because you are under stress or because you feel unhappy and tired, you are more prone to illness and disease. Your attitude will often be negative and you will have a hard time dealing with life's challenges. Which is the essence of the soul; When a person dies, he leaves the body.

Lesson 4: How Reiki Works

The human body is made up of more than 50 trillion cells. Every cell contains omniscient wisdom and is connected with the universe and every living thing in it. A good analogy is to think of the universe as one big ocean of water. Every living thing in that ocean is like a tiny droplet. Together these droplets form and are part of Reiki, the universal life force.

Reiki is part of our genetic makeup. Built-in intelligence that energizes the mind, body, and spirit. Reiki stimulates growth, health, life as well as healing. When allowed to circulate freely around the body, it can keep us alive and healthy for more than one hundred and twenty years.

Unfortunately, bad habits and bad choices cause the Reiki flow to suffocate. It is important to remember that Reiki cannot be destroyed. It continues to exist as part of the universe even when

When mind-body and spirit are in harmony, the biological intelligence intensifies, which manages the body's resources and allows the body to heal itself and function properly. Reiki is the key to revealing the optimum abilities of the body. The seven main energy centers in the body control the flow of the universal life force. They are called chakras. Each chakra is responsible for providing energy to certain parts of the body. When they are blocked or blocked, the body becomes sick and the energy flow is diluted.

A complete Reiki treatment reopens the chakras and rebalances the flow of universal life force throughout the body. To increase the flow of Reiki energy, a person will normally need four complete treatments over four consecutive days. This will activate the body's immune system and natural healing abilities. Normally, the body starts by cleansing itself of toxins. As the poisons dissipate, the body rebalances and the healing process can begin

Many cultures have developed techniques and disciplines that stimulate the flow of KI energy in the body. But Reiki is the easiest.

The 7 Major Chakra Points

The Crown Chakra (white or violet) is positioned on the top of the head. It represents enlightenment, intuition and spiritual vision. Energy supply to the pineal glands, upper brain and right eye.

The Third Eye Chakra (Indigo) is positioned in the middle of the forehead, just above the eyebrows. It represents psychic perception, telepathy and ESP. Energy supply to the spine, lower brain, left eye, pituitary gland, nose, ears and central nervous system.

The Throat Chakra (light blue) is positioned in the centre of the neck It represents self expression, emotions, communication and creativity. Energy supply to the throat, thyroid gland, upper lungs, arms and digestive tract.

The Heart Chakra (rose and green) is positioned in the middle of the chest. It represents emotions, love, devotion, spiritual growth and compassion. Energy supply to the heart, thymus gland, liver, lungs and the circulation system.

The Solar Plexus Chakra (yellow) is positioned just above the naval. It represents the centre of the body, food is assimilated, turned into energy and distributed throughout the body. Energy supply to the emotions, stomach, liver, digestion, gall bladder and the pancreas.

The Sacral Chakra (orange) is positioned just below the naval. It represents sexual energy, perceptions and first impressions of people. Energy supply to the reproductive organs, legs and the glands.

The Root Chakra (red) is positioned at the genitals. It represents life, physical vitality, birth and creation. Energy supply to the spine, kidneys, bladder and the suprarenal glands.

Reiki is always present in our bodies. This means that anyone can tap into this deeply available intelligent energy for healing.
However, if you are not in tune with the universal life force, you will only use about 10-20% of its capacity for healing.
Takata explains it best when she describes Reiki as being like radio waves. We cannot see them but we know they are everywhere around us. When we turn on the radio and tune in to the radio waves, we can receive a signal. That signal is converted into a radio program. Similarly, cosmic life force is everywhere, although we cannot see it unless we use Kirlian photography.
When we are energized by a Reiki Master, it allows us to tap into Reiki to heal ourselves and others. This gift of healing will stay with us for the rest of our lives. We can only lose it if we use it for negative or destructive purposes. Reiki is pure and should be treated as such.

Section Three

Lesson 5: The 5 Reiki Principles

Just for today, I won't worry. Just for today, I won't be angry. Just for today, I will do my job honestly. Just for today, I will give thanks for my many blessings. Just for today, I will be kind to my neighbors and all my creatures.

The Reiki principles are spiritual ideals. By applying these precepts, you will add balance and substance to your life. You must realize that you are not expected to live every moment of your life within the framework of these ideals. As humans, we are all imperfect, and that's why each principle begins with «Just for today.» You may not feel pressured or stressed in your daily efforts to improve yourself. If you fail today, you can always start over tomorrow. The more you work with principles, the more likely you are to apply them as a way of life.

To become more familiar with the Reiki principles, you should read them aloud at
You can then place the copy in a prominent place where you're sure to see it every day, or if you're going to practice Reiki professionally, put it in the healing room. The five principles of Reiki mean different things to each of us. Meditation will help open your awareness.

Just sit or lie in a comfortable position and close your eyes. Repeat one of those ideals over and over and use it like a mantra. When you enter a meditative state, you will become aware of what is happening inside your mind and body. You may experience many different feelings, emotions, and thoughts. If you do this exercise in a group, share your experiences and write down everything that happened during the meditation. It is interesting to regularly look at your notes on this exercise to see how mature you are in applying these precepts. Repeat the meditation practice each year and compare notes or if in a group discuss the differences that have occurred.

Just For Today I Will Not Worry

Worry causes stress and anxiety leading to an imbalance of the mind-body and spirit and blockage to the root chakra.

The best way to overcome worry is to accept that all of us are faced with difficulties and setbacks in our lives. How we respond to them determines how we ultimately lead our lives.
If you choose to respond negatively by getting upset and anxious towards one of life's setbacks you have chosen to damage the balance of your mind body and spirit.
If you respond positively by accepting the setback as an opportunity to learn you can live a happier and more fulfilling life

Taking time to do something fun every day is very important and it will make you happy. Laughter can bring us healing and also make us more positive about our lives. It can also help prevent some diseases, as stress has proven to be the number one cause of most illnesses and even death.
Use Reiki to rebalance your mind and spirit and increase your determination. Put one hand on the root chakra and the other hand on the heart chakra. Reiki will bring your mind body and soul into balance. Keep your hands on these chakra points for as long as you intuitively feel you need them. This Reiki technique will clear blockages caused by stress, worry , and anxiety.
 It can be used for self-healing or on another person.
.

Just For Today I Will Not Be Angry

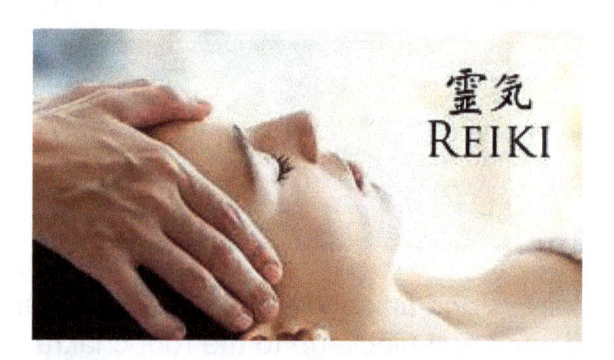

Anger is an emotion. When we get angry, we lose control of that emotion. To live by the above principle, we must understand what triggers our anger and how we can choose to remove this destructive emotion from our being.

This simple implementation allows you to take back control of your emotions, and as such, you can now choose to respond positively to the situation, rather than react negatively.

Every time you meet someone, energy is exchanged. If you are both happy and find the meeting pleasant, then the energy exchange is neutral. However, if.

Anger is the answer of choice. Decide every day not to let negative people or situations steal your energy. At the physical level, anger can cause stomach and digestive disorders. Choose to live a healthier life without anger.

Help the balancing process with Reiki. Place one hand on the chakra of the third eye and the other hand on the root chakra. Keep your hands there as long as you intuitively feel it is necessary. This reiki technique will help you control and eliminate this destructive emotion. It can be used for self-medication or another person

.

Just For Today I Will Do My Work Honestly

誠
実

Honesty

Integrity means different things to different people. Many people think it's fine to take a few pens from the office to the home, the company making millions in profits each year just to be able to afford to lose a few stationery items.
Everyone is dishonest at some point. You cannot steal from another person or company, but rather from yourself.

To use Reiki to help rebalance this principle, place one hand on the third eye chakra and the other hand on the solar plexus chakra. Keep your hands there for as long as you intuitively think they should stay in these chakra points. This additional hand position can be used to heal yourself or other people.

Just For Today I Will Give Thanks For My Many Blessings

Life tends to give us what we need, it may not be what we want, but it will be what we need.

If we understand these lessons and grow accordingly, we will become spiritually enlightened. Instead of wasting life complaining about things that have happened to you and the problems you face.

Retreat regularly for a moment and discover and appreciate the many blessings in your life.

Make a list of all your blessings. You will be amazed at how many wonderful things to thank. Set aside materialistic things. They are superficial and meaningless. Pay attention to things that are free and bring joy and humility to your life. For example, your mind, body, spirit, health, family, friends, flowers, trees, sea, sun, love, faith, knowledge, landscape, animals, birds, etc., the list is endless.

Place one hand on the chakra of the third eye and the other hand on the occiput. Use Reiki to balance this principle in your life or the life of another person.

.

Just For Today I Will Be Kind to My Neighbour and Every Living Thing

The law of karma says that what is happening is coming. Send love and in return, you will receive love. Send a favor and you will get a favor. Submit healing and you will receive healing. Distribute positive thoughts and get positive results.

Karma is a sword with two edges. Send out negative thoughts and get negative results. Living in this prescription will give you a happier and less stressful life full of joy, peace, and love.

To achieve this principle of balance for yourself or others, first, place one hand on the chakra of the third eye and the other hand on the root chakra. When you feel ready, move your hand from the chakra of the third eye to the chakra and move your hand from the root chakra to the heart chakra and keep it there until you intuitively feel that you are finished.

It is important to remember that the Reiki principles are only guides for a happier and more fulfilling life. Use meditation to unlock the true meaning of these precepts and incorporate them into your life. They will transform your life.

The 5 Reiki Principles are not commandments; they are simply gifts of wisdom.

Section Four

Lesson 6: Preparing For Reiki 1

Many students start as skeptics just curious to learn more and leave as Reiki enthusiasts. The secret to getting the most out of Reiki is to be open to Reiki. Instead of being negative and skeptical, let the joy of Reiki envelop you. Leave your fears and doubts behind and dive headfirst into a life-changing experience. Reiki draws you to itself. If you are attending the first degree Reiki seminar/workshop, you are there for a reason - you need it. Trust the omniscient wisdom of Reiki. Remember you will
.need the First Degree attunement once in your life, so make it a celebration you will never forget. It's up to you.

The Initiation Ceremony

First of all, let's talk for a moment about Reiki initiation. By definition, Reiki initiation is a process/technique performed by the Reiki teacher to activate the Reiki symbols introduced into the energy field of the student at the level of the head and middle of the palms.
It is a complex technique that involves good breathing control

It also means that the state of health of the student's energy field may allow easy harmonization or may hinder the harmonization process to some extent.
For example, if a Reiki student has different negative energies in their aura which have created energetic blockages, tensions, then during harmonization when the teacher tries to activate Reiki symbols and certain energetic meridians these blockages can hinder this process.

- Avoid alcohol for at least a week. Instead, drink more natural juice full of vitamins and minerals.
- If possible avoid smoking for at least 1 week to allow the energy meridians of your lungs to improve.
- Regarding the foods you eat, try not to eat anything heavy the evening before the class. It is said that once a person will become vegetarian, then in ~ 7 years the quality of their energy will improve so much that naturally, they will start to manifest healing abilities. Having a healthy diet will keep you healthy and will be a plus when trying to help others.
- Have a good night's sleep (at least 8 hours) before the Reiki class.

After the Initiation
After restoring Reiki, it will take 2 to 3 weeks for the changes in the energy field to stabilize. During those 2 to 3 weeks, students are encouraged to practice their own Reiki treatments. In this way, they will improve the state of their energy field. Then you can also work on others. You will also experience symptoms as you go through withdrawal. This whole process will take about 21 days or so.
During this phase of purification, physical, emotional, mental, and energetic will detox toxins and negative programs that have formed or built up over time and will bring about positive changes

#1 Physical

Although the Reiki attunement is quite passive for the practitioner, there are a few "side effects" for the students.
For instance, some people feel certain sensations in their feet or hands, like – coolness, heat, buzzing, or tingling. Additionally, some will experience:
- heaviness in limbs;
- diarrhea;
- blurred vision;
- runny nose;
- cranial pressure;
- headaches – some people will experience just a dull head ache the first couple of days after their attunement, some have complained of migraines for several weeks after the attunement, and some don't experience any headaches at all;
- chest pain.

Note – the more toxins there are in your body, the more side effects you can expect to experience.

#2 Emotional

Another effect is an increase in moodiness. You may become more emotional than is usually normal for you.
For example, you may experience:
- sadness;
- crying without cause;
- frustration;
- fear;
- anger outbursts.

Why does this happen?
The deep emotions and traumas that have been suppressed may come back or get worse before gradually fading away.
For unresolved emotions to fade away, they have to go through you. When these past emotions reappear, it can lead to anger, sadness, depression, or fear.
If these are the emotions you feel after a Reiki initiation, rest assured that they are normal. Don't panic and blame yourself for it.

Note – on a positive note, I can assure you that this emotional detox is temporary.

#3 Energetical

As for the higher attunement of reiki, the practitioner naturally begins to release deeper buried negative energy from his body.
When your body releases and releases the energy it held, that energy is always sprayed on the sinks and counters as it washes away forever.
After completing this process, most students will almost immediately notice higher vibrations in their bodies.
When you are on a high vibration, one of the problems is that some people will act like energy vampires and try to knock you down.
But you will no longer tolerate those who suck up your positive energy. Drama doesn't appeal to you and you don't want it part of your life.
While it's not easy, you'll find that you're setting boundaries you've never set before, and you're even ending friendships.
You may also realize that toxic energy will slow down your spiritual

Important note – when you are at a high vibration, you shine so brightly that you can attract the attention of lower vibrational entities (in the astral world) who are drawn to you like a moth to a flame. You are most vulnerable when going to sleep.
Tip – before going to sleep, set the intention that during sleep you will only be visited by angels or spiritual masters.

#4 Changed Spiritual Beliefs

Giving and receiving Reiki is a spiritual experience, not a religion. You don't have to adopt any beliefs to practice it. However, after being restored to Reiki, you may have a new spiritual belief system. The first belief that changes after it pays off is the belief that you are just your ego, that your ego is the person you've identified your whole life, thinking this is you.

.

#5 Radical Shifts

Once tuned, your vibrations will increase and radical shifts can occur in your life, because when you change your vibrations, what you resonate in will change.
For example, you may notice a change in your career. Many people even start businesses as life coaches or healers of some kind. When they know they came here for a greater purpose, they can't spend another second in a soul-crushing job.
You feel compelled to do your part on Earth.
Your humanitarian nature is calling you. In addition, you feel a connection and empathy with plants, animals and living beings. You may also notice that you are beginning to be attracted to moving to another place to live.
.

Note – you may notice these things since they just simply don't resonate anymore.

Final Words

To reduce your chance of side effects after a Reiki attunement, it is recommended to:

- avoid caffeinated drinks (for at least a week before attunement) since caffeine causes the mind to be over-active; caffeine can be found in coffee, some sodas (like Pepsi and Coca Cola), energy drinks, some teas, weight loss supplements, and cocoa;
- have a regular diet high in fruits and vegetables;
- avoid high protein food, especially animal-based protein;
- do not smoke or consume alcohol;

Ways to Use Reiki after the Attunement

Once you have been attuned to Reiki, the energy will flow through your hands whenever you touch it with the intention of healing or helping. You can use Reiki on:

- Yourself
- Other Adults
- children
- Prenatal babies
- Accidents
- Emergencies
- Animals
- Birds
- Fish
- Plants
- Trees
- Seeds
- Crystals
- Food
- Drinks
- Your work
- Contracts
- Projects
- Letters
- Documents
- Your car
- For protection
- Travelling
- Your home
- Drinking water
- Bath water
- Shower water

The list is endless, you are only limited by your imagination!

Section Five

Lesson 7: Anatomic Illustrations for Reiki

With its infinite wisdom, Reiki goes to the place in the body that requires healing. That's why Reiki is very easy to learn and practice. There is no need to study the anatomy of the human body or animals to successfully treat a human or animal. Just place your hands on the body and channel the energy. Reiki takes care of the rest.

However, it can be helpful to know where the main organs in the body, the lymphatic and endocrine systems, are located. This knowledge will allow you to treat specific problems or organs quickly and easily.

The following illustrations are simple diagrams of human anatomy. If you decide to further your studies, we recommend making full use of your public library. They will have books on human anatomy as well as on the anatomy of various pets and animals. Of course,

The Endocrine System

What is the Endocrine System?

The endocrine system, also known as the hormone system, is found in all mammals, birds, fish, and many other types of living organisms.

Hormones are made by the glands and are released into the blood or fluid surrounding the cells; and

receptors in different organs and tissues that recognize and respond to hormones.

Why Are Hormones Important?

Hormones act as chemical messengers that are released into the bloodstream and act on an organ in another part of the body. Although hormones reach all parts of the body, only target cells with compatible receptors are equipped to respond. More than 50 hormones have been identified in humans and other vertebrates. Hormones control or regulate many biological processes and are often produced in the body in extremely low amounts.

- blood sugar control (insulin);
- differentiation, growth, and function of reproductive organs (testosterone (T) and estradiol); and
- body growth and energy production (growth hormone and thyroid hormone).

Like a lock and key, many hormones work by binding to receptors made in cells. When a hormone binds to a receptor, the receptor carries out the hormone's instructions, either by changing the cell's existing proteins or activating genes that will make a new protein. The hormone-receptor complex turns on or off specific biological processes in cells, tissues, and organs.

Some examples of hormones include:
- Estrogens are the group of hormones responsible for female sexual development. They are produced primarily by the ovaries and in small amounts by the adrenal glands.
- Androgens are responsible for male sex characteristics. Testosterone, the sex hormone produced by the testicles, is an androgen.
- The thyroid gland secretes two main hormones, thyroxine and triiodothyronine, into the bloodstream. These thyroid hormones stimulate all the cells in the body and control biological processes such as growth, reproduction, development, and metabolism.

The endocrine system, made up of different hormones of the whole body, regulates all biological processes in the body, from fertilization to adulthood and old age, including the development of the brain and nervous system, and the growth and function of the reproductive system. like metabolism and blood sugar levels. The female ovaries, male testicles and pituitary, thyroid and adrenal glands are the main components of the endocrine system.

Where are Endocrine Glands Located in the Human Body?

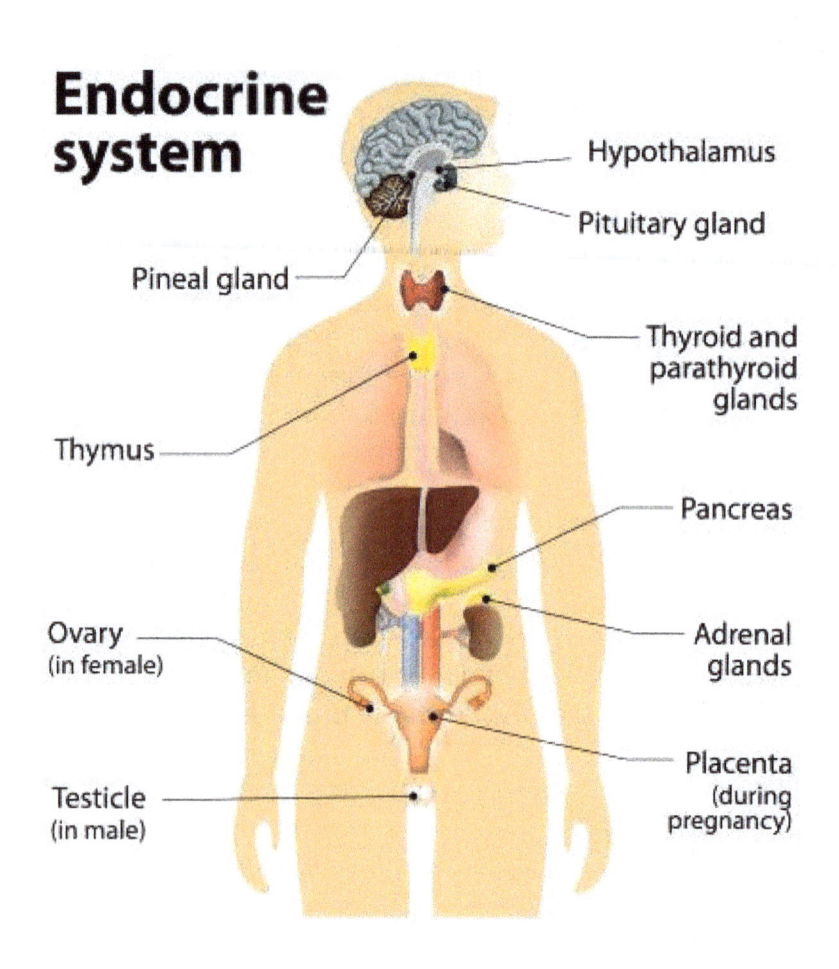

Endocrine system

- Hypothalamus
- Pituitary gland
- Pineal gland
- Thyroid and parathyroid glands
- Thymus
- Pancreas
- Ovary (in female)
- Adrenal glands
- Testicle (in male)
- Placenta (during pregnancy)

Hypothalamus - The hypothalamus links our endocrine and nervous systems together. The hypothalamus drives the endocrine system.
Pituitary gland - The pituitary gland receives signals from the hypothalamus. This gland has two lobes, the posterior and anterior lobes. The posterior lobe secretes hormones that are made by the hypothalamus. The anterior lobe produces its hormones, several of which act on other endocrine glands.
Thyroid gland - The thyroid gland is critical to the healthy development and maturation of vertebrates and regulates metabolism.
Adrenal glands - The adrenal gland is made up of two glands: the cortex and medulla. These glands produce hormones in response to stress and regulate blood pressure, glucose metabolism, and the body's salt and water balance.
Pancreas - The pancreas is responsible for producing glucagon and insulin. Both hormones help regulate the concentration of glucose (sugar) in the blood.
Gonads - The male reproductive gonads, or testes, and female reproductive gonads, or ovaries, produce steroids that affect growth and development and also regulate reproductive cycles and behaviors. The major categories of gonadal steroids are androgens,

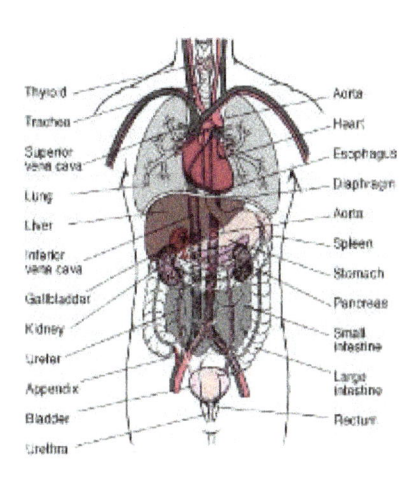

The Lymphatic System

Lymphatic system, a subsystem of the circulatory system of the vertebrate body that consists of a complex network of vessels, tissues, and organs. The lymphatic system helps maintain water balance in the body by collecting excess fluid and particles in the tissues and depositing them in the bloodstream. It also helps defend the body against infections by supplying anti-disease cells called lymphocytes. This article focuses on the human lymphatic system.

Lymphatic circulation
The lymphatic system can be considered an essential drainage system because, as blood circulates through the body, plasma leaks into the tissues through the thin walls of the capillaries. The part of plasma that escapes is called the interstitial or extracellular fluid, and it contains oxygen, glucose, amino acids, and other nutrients needed by tissue cells. Although most of this fluid seeps right back into the bloodstream, one percent of it, along with particulate matter, is left behind. The lymphatic system removes this fluid and these materials from the tissues, returns them through the lymphatic vessels into the bloodstream, and thus prevents fluid imbalances that lead to the death of the organism

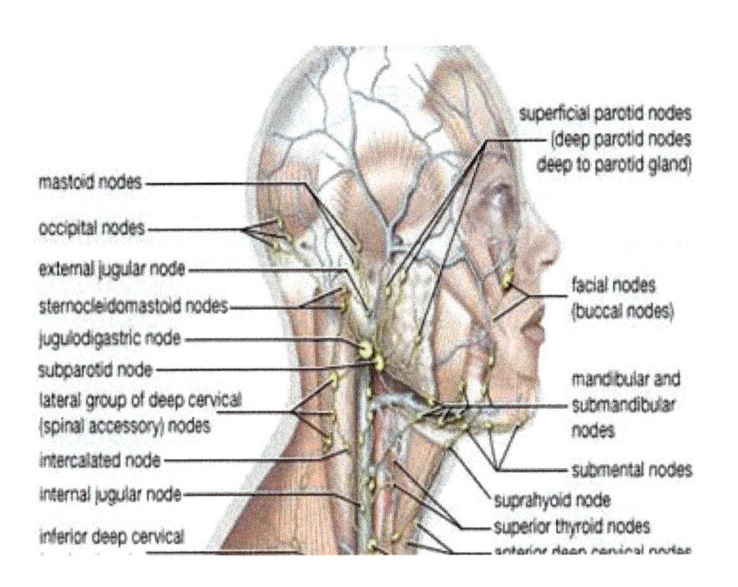

- mastoid nodes
- occipital nodes
- external jugular node
- sternocleidomastoid nodes
- jugulodigastric node
- subparotid node
- lateral group of deep cervical (spinal accessory) nodes
- intercalated node
- internal jugular node
- inferior deep cervical

- superficial parotid nodes (deep parotid nodes deep to parotid gland)
- facial nodes (buccal nodes)
- mandibular and submandibular nodes
- submental nodes
- suprahyoid node
- superior thyroid nodes
- anterior deep cervical nodes

Section Six

Lesson 8: Reiki Self Treatment

Once you have received your first level remuneration, from a Reiki Master, you are ready to work with global vitality. However, you must realize that for every profession, it is necessary to practice and master the skills involved in healing first. Madam Takata taught her students how to heal themselves first, then their families, then their friends. Only then will she believe that they will have the qualifications and ability to work as a practitioner and heal others.

When a person first learns to drive a car, they need time, practice, and experience to master what appears to be a rather complicated set of procedures. However, in a relatively short period of time, they can safely and easily drive the car as they unconsciously control the car and all the different skills involved in driving. Likewise, with time, practice, and experience, you will master the skills and techniques involved in the healing art of Reiki. Treat the first few months as a learning experience, almost like an apprenticeship; This will give you the time needed to develop your confidence and skills. Remember that the more you work with Reiki,

Self-healing is the starting point for personal growth and self-discovery. Reiki is not just a tool for healing; It also offers personal protection, prevention and transformation on all levels. As you move forward on your new path, you will inevitably face setbacks and setbacks in life that are often like an entire coast, but with Reiki you will have the strength to deal with them. them as if they were just pebbles on the beach. Even if you never use Reiki to heal anyone but yourself, you will find a new sense of balance and

No other self-treatment is as simple and effective as Reiki. Because Reiki is always there for you, whenever you feel tired, stressed, aching, you can soothe them by placing your hands on yourself. Reiki's infinite wisdom will go wherever it is needed. Recharge your batteries every day, not just when problems, difficulties, worries or illnesses arise. Daily self-treatment will help prevent illness and disease, bringing your life back into focus and balance quickly. Every time you use Reiki on yourself, you increase your self-esteem and self-love. You will discover your mission in life and become more compassionate and loving. Instead of stressing over normal things you come into contact with every day like traffic jams; meetings, interviews, doctor or dentist visits, waiting lines, the children you need and your family responsibilities but a few, allow Reiki to come into your life and let Reiki become a new way of life for you

Take a little time each day to self-medicate. The first thing in the morning will give you a positive motivation for the new day. In addition, self-treatment at night will help you relax and be comfortable, leading to a good night's sleep. Good places to treat yourself are in the bath, shower, or lying in bed. The possibilities are endless and the benefits are immeasurable.

Reiki is a gift to be savored and enjoyed. Remember the more you use Reiki the stronger and more profound it becomes. Daily use could extend your own life by several years.

HOW REIKI CAN HELP YOU

There are several benefits to be gained, which occur without any effort from a daily Reiki self-treatment including:

Reiki influences Intuition
Besides helping reduce pain the emotional benefits can have far-reaching effects as well. Sometimes we aren't able to use our intuition because our third eye is blocked or we aren't able to communicate with spirit because another chakra is blocked and energy isn't flowing into it.
Our minds may be unable to communicate with higher realms of consciousness because our energy could be stuck. This can block creativity or even hamper us from being able to open to love and intimacy.
Let's talk about money though. It's something we all need and it's an important part of life. If your root chakra is blocked, shrunken, or overactive, you may be having financial problems, problems finding a stable living situation, or landing a good job.
Reiki can Unblock Chakras
Reiki can help unblock this chakra and while it's not going to rain money down from the sky, you may suddenly think of a new idea, something you can follow up with, or someone you know that can help you.
Sometimes our root chakra is imbalanced because the other two chakras above it are blocked so we have no ideas, no manifesting power, and no confidence. All the chakras need to be running like a circuit for our life to be balanced.
Sometimes our financial strife can come from not speaking up for ourselves and so a clear throat chakra would be essential in our success as well.
Reiki for Love
Let's talk about love, it's on our minds and sometimes feels out of reach right? Maybe we have gotten into a habitual way of thinking about ourselves or relationships that is keeping our guard up or keeping us from being open to new experiences.
That block would be in the heart chakra. Reiki can help with that too. Perhaps we are severing ties in our interpersonal relationships at work, with friends or coworkers, and an old would be making us reactive or closed off from people unnecessarily

Renew Energy and Release Baggage with Reiki
Reiki is a great way to take out the emotional garbage and don't worry if you have a lot, reiki isn't exhaustible, it's a renewable energy source.
If you have become fear-based or rigid in your thinking and perhaps become anti-social or pessimistic, reiki can help with that too. Often our belief systems that we inherit from our parents can be unanchored from our psyche with the gentle nudging of this. Maybe we have been holding onto guilt for something we did a long time ago and we do not feel deserving. Reiki can help us recognize which traumas are still affecting our perceptions of the world and holding us back.
Perhaps it's as simple as an attitude we have developed that gives us a sourness and repelling people from wanting to engage with us. Imagine if you could shift your energetic state so that people

HOW TO TREAT YOURSELF WITH REIKI

There is no right or wrong way to work with Reiki on oneself. As you become more experienced with the Reiki energy you will intuitively move your hands to wherever it feels right. However, if you are aware of a specific problem such as an injury or pain, then you should place your hands directly over that area, to begin with, and follow up with full self-treatment.
In the beginning, it is always best to follow a set procedure as shown in the following illustrations marked "Self Treatment Hand Positions".
When you have mastered the hand positions you can then leave each self-treatment up to your intuition. You may wish to work with music to add the right relaxing mood. Find a place where you won't be disturbed if possible. Normally you would spend three to five minutes on each position.

However, time is often short; but remember a little Reiki is better than no Reiki. On completion of the self-treatment drink a large glass of purified water. Close your eyes and go inside and pay attention to the thoughts and emotions that have arisen during the session. You may feel light-headed, and if you need to rest, or sit down for a short time, allow yourself this time.

If you feel you need to continue to work on a specific area of the body, even if you have completed a full self-treatment, then go with your intuition; always listen to your mind and body.

Remember the following hand positions are only a guide – Use your intuition

SELF TREATMENT HAND POSITIONS

First position: Palms of your hands are placed against your face, cupping your hands over your eyes lightly and fingers upon your forehead. No pressure needed - touch lightly!

Image: Step-By-Step Reiki (Carmen Fernandez)

Second position: Place your hands on your temples to help to clear an overactive or tired mind. You can also treat your ears and jaw muscles in this way. A nice tip is to rest your elbows on your knees for support.

Image: Step-By-Step Reiki (Carmen Fernandez)

Third position: Move your hands to the back of your head and neck area. This will relieve any tension and is refreshing to the mind. This may be more comfortable if you are seated in a comfy

Image: Step-By-Step Reiki (Carmen Fernandez)

Fourth position: Move your hands to either side of your neck now. This is especially beneficial to the thyroid area. It is also excellent for communication and self-expression.

Image: Step-By-Step Reiki (Carmen Fernandez)

Fifth position: Place your hands above your breasts on either side of your chest. This is a great way to enable lymph drainage, which in turn removes any toxin from the body.

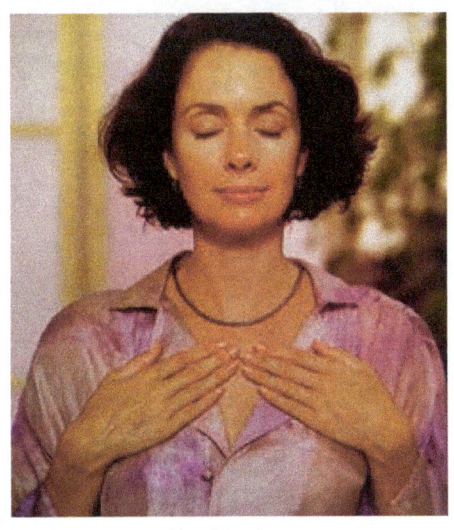

Image: Step-By-Step Reiki (Carmen Fernandez)

Sixth position: Place your hands just below the breasts, fingers gently touching. This helps when dealing with emotions, both the heart chakra and solar plexus chakra are treated in this area.

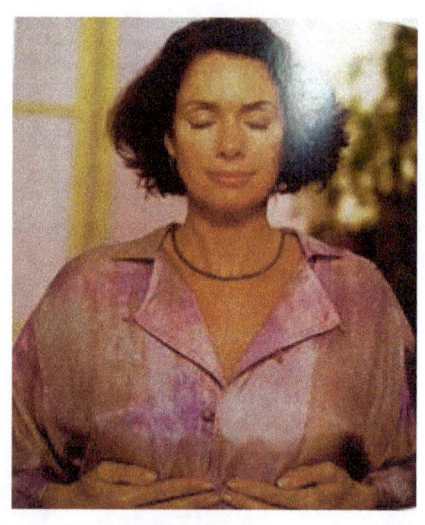

Image: Step-By-Step Reiki (Carmen Fernandez)

Seventh position: Moving downwards, rest your hands over your ribcage. This will stimulate the solar plexus and all surrounding

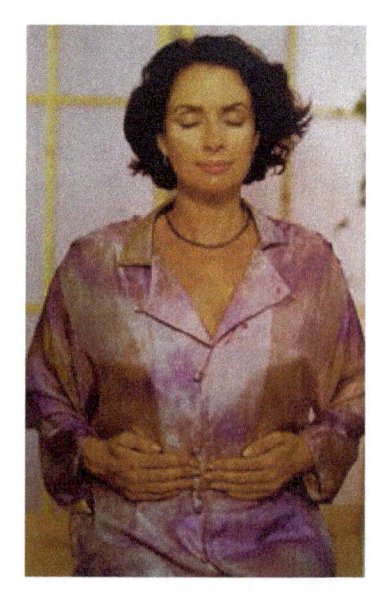

Image: Step-By-Step Reiki (Carmen Fernandez)

Eighth position: Place your hands just below your navel. This is excellent for releasing sexual tension and treats the spleen. When this chakra is open it enables and allows creativity to flow

Image: Step-By-Step Reiki (Carmen Fernandez)

Ninth position: Place your hands on each shoulder now. This will benefit the neck, shoulders and back. You can also cross your arms over each other if that feels a bit more comfortable.

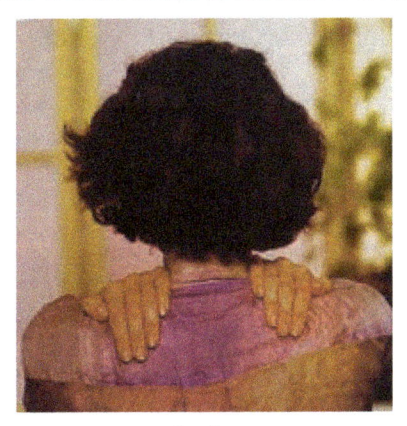

Image: Step-By-Step Reiki (Carmen Fernandez)

Tenth position: Cross your arms. Place one hand on your shoulder and the other on your rib cage. This allows the reiki energy to flow downward.

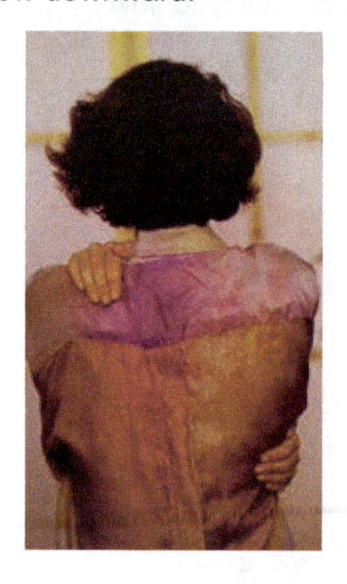

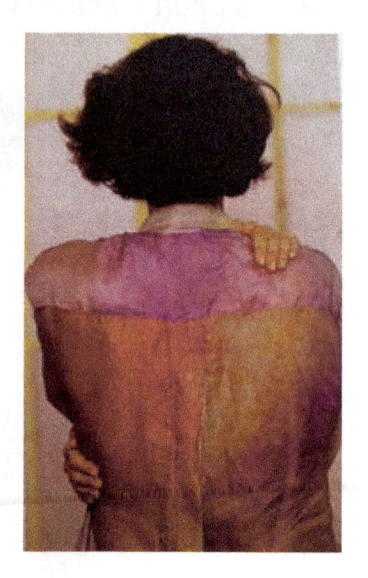

Repeat the movement on the other side of your body. Image: Step-By-Step Reiki (Carmen Fernandez)

Eleventh position: Move your hands to your lower back now and place them over your kidneys. This treats all organs in this area including the adrenal glands.

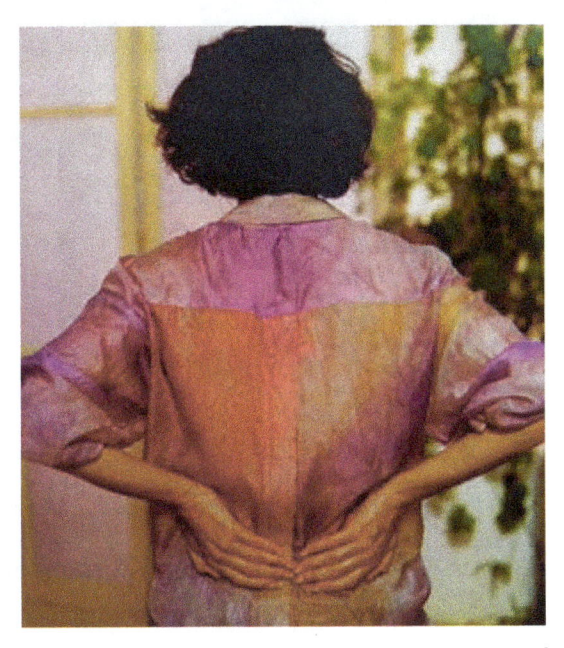

Image: Step-By-Step Reiki (Carmen Fernandez)

Twelfth position: Lastly move your hands to the lower back to the base of the spine. This will stimulate the fight or flight response in the body and enables us to function and allows us to survive in our surroundings.

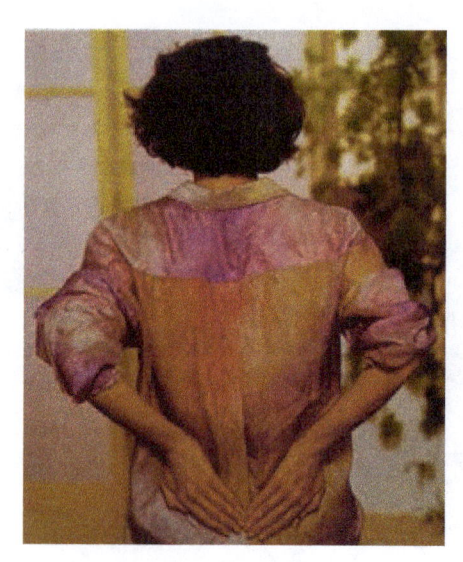

Image: Step-By-Step Reiki (Carmen Fernandez)

To end off this self Reiki session you can gently rub your feet. This will enable grounding, and also releases any residual tension. You can also place one hand on the forehead (Third Eye Chakra), and one at the base of your spine (Root Chakra).

Section Seven

Lesson 9: Preparing To Treat Others with Reiki

In today's age, our clients are very clued up when it comes to just about anything. The internet has given access to everything you can imagine. I mean I could be one YouTube video away from being a brain surgeon. The same can be said for your clients. They will ask questions and you must be prepared to supply the correct answers as they will have a general knowledge anyway. As a practitioner, it is vital to have certain things in place when setting up a practice. I will now take you through some of the steps needed to provide a safe and secure environment for you and your clients.

So you started a Reiki practice. WHAT NOW?!?

It can be quite scary when you first start. What if you do something wrong? What if your client hates you? What if it doesn't work? What if? What if? What if?

Firstly, take a breath. All this stressing is not helping. Let's look at

12 Steps To Creating Your Reiki Treatment Room

Step 1 – Create a gentle safe place for the treatment. You can use a treatment couch or a table with a thick blanket on top. A cushion for under the legs is also a good idea as this will support the back. If you do not have a table then a chair will suffice.

Step 2 – Ensure the temperature in the room is comfortable. Make sure you have a warm blanket at the ready to cover the person you are working on as the body loses heat during healing. Remember to talk to your client. Ask them if they are too hot or too cold.

Step 3 – Avoid bright or glaring light directly above the bed or table. Soft, ambient lighting is always more soothing.

Step 4 – Have a box of tissues available. Emotions can be releases so watch out for tears.

Step 5 – It is important to protect yourself to ensure that you do not absorb the recipient's emotional emissions. This is as simple as imagining you are surrounded by a protective white or purple shield, bubble, or light.

Step 6 – Play soft background music to ease people into a state of relaxation.

Step 7 – Avoid sudden interruptions. Switch off your mobile device, television and make sure the dog is resting.

Step 8 – Wash your hands thoroughly and clean your nails. I always recommend using a few drops of essential oil such as lavender on your hands as they will be coming close to people's faces.

Step 9 – Be mindful of smells. Avoid heavy perfumes, eating garlic beforehand, or cigarette smoke.

Step 10 – Check that the recipient does not mind you touching him or her. If they do not like to be touched, you can try hovering your hands slightly above the body.

Step 11 – Ask if they have any other health problems before giving a treatment.

Step 12 – Aim to cover different areas for about 5 minutes each and see if you can notice any sensations in your hands.

Now that you have your practice set up and clients are booking treatments with you, it is very important to have the following documentation in place.

Client Consent Form

This one is incredibly important. As you are working with people, you need to have their permission to perform treatments. I was working as a massage therapist for many years and one day a colleague had a client in for a massage. My colleague being a male massage therapist, always ensured he had his clients fill in the consent forms before ANY treatment, and rightfully so. One day a policeman showed up to arrest him for assault on a female client. Long story, short as she had permitted for him to do the treatment, no charges were made and all ended well, but you can see how easy it is to fall into serious trouble very quickly. The consent form is more to ensure you don't get into any sticky situations such as this. You will find as part of the course I will include the forms but feel free to create your own as you grow in your business.

Client Information Form

This one is equally important. How can you treat a client or offer a service if you have no history or information on your client? The simple answer is, you can't.

This form will have information such as contact information, medical history, medications being used, and any other relevant information you may need to offer the best treatment possible. But most importantly is to LISTEN TO YOUR CLIENT. More often than not, the client will start telling you about things they failed to list on the information forms. Maybe things like they are stressed due to a work situation or miserable in their current relationships. These bits of information will help you with your healing session. Furthermore, your client will appreciate the added attention to detail you show them.

Information Brochure

This one may seem irrelevant and a waste of money. But let's say you have a new client who is unsure, giving her something to read in the comfort of her home might be all she needs to make that booking. Never over-promise though. Always be straight with your client. She will appreciate the honesty and keep coming back as she won't have unrealistic expectations. She may even refer a friend or six to you in the future so always be real with clients

How To Prepare Your Client

To prepare your client for a Reiki session, contact them a day or two before their appointment. This is to confirm the appointment and also to remind them to wear comfy clothing etc. but we will look into this more.

Get Relaxed

About 30 minutes before the session, advise your client to take some time to sit and relax by themselves. Take this time to enjoy some quiet, whether this is in a room by or in the parking lot in their car as they wait to go in.
Close your eyes and take some deep breaths, and they can even consider taking the time to meditate before your session. Listening to guided meditation will also help for that extra relaxation.
Overall, the goal of Reiki is to heal, so by going in with a clear head, you can guarantee that you will not be distracted and stressed out throughout the session.

Ensure the client is hydrated. Reiki sessions can be up to an hour or more in length and the client will be incredibly thirsty if they have not had something to drink. Having said this it is also important that they use the restroom before the session.
Ensuring that you either have room to do your session in or a space that you will not be disturbed in is important. Take some time before your session to let others in your house know that you would like to be given some privacy for the next hour or so.

Ensure that you have somewhere in your space that you can lay down, whether it's on a couch or a blanket on the ground. Whatever you choose, make sure you will be comfortable laying there for anywhere from 20-90 minutes (depending on your session length).

You also may want to have a speaker near you to play some calming music or sounds of nature. This is optional, of course, and you may want silence instead.

While there are no set-in-stone rules to what should happen before a Reiki session takes place and with that said, no mandatory place for it to happen, it's always best to consider some things to make sure you get the most healing out of your session

The Treatment

Remove All Jewellery

Reiki can travel through all materials such as stone, brick, concrete, and metal. However, the metal and stones used in the manufacture of jewelry come into contact with and attract certain types of negative energy. To enable you to work with Reiki free from all subtle energy disturbances it is advisable to remove all jewelry such as rings, watches, earrings, chains, and necklaces. Therapists who work with precious stones and crystals for healing recognize that these materials can become saturated with negative energy. That is why they cleanse them regularly.

Remove Tight Clothing

To allow Reiki to flow freely through you and your client you both must remove tight clothing such as belts, ties, and shoes. This will also make you feel more comfortable and relaxed. Reiki can travel through clothes so there is no need to remove any other forms of

Avoid Alcohol

Alcohol dissipates energy. Always refrain from consuming alcohol if you know you are going to be working with Reiki for at least twenty-four hours before a session.

Personal Hygiene

Ensure you smell and appear clean and fresh. Avoid wearing strong perfumes or aftershaves. If you smoke make sure you brush your teeth or use a mouth freshener. Refrain from eating garlic, onions, or any other food that may leave a smell on your breath.

Wash your hands before a Reiki session using a lightly scented or neutral soap. Your hands come into contact with your client's face and skin so it is important for hygiene purposes and the peace of mind of your client to have clean hands

The Invocation

It is important to remember that as a Reiki practitioner you are not healing your clients. The people receiving Reiki are healing themselves. You are merely the channel that enables them to draw the Reiki energy through your hands to the place it is needed. The invocation is a token that symbolizes you are giving up any claims to power. You simply place your hands on their shoulders for the invocation

An Example of a Personal Invocation

We always like to take a few moments before we begin a treatment to mentally prepare ourselves for working as a channel for Reiki. This quiet time is perfect for getting in touch with our guides, mentors, and assistants. It allows us a brief moment of reflection and focuses our thoughts on healing. It is important to begin the treatment with the right mental attitude. Your wish should be to pass on unconditional love and healing in the purest form and sense.

I ask that the power and wisdom of Reiki permit me to become a channel for Reiki's unconditional love and healing on behalf of_____ (insert clients name) may Reiki's infinite wisdom go exactly where it is needed most, should it be for their higher good. May we all be empowered by your divine love and blessing -Amen."

Cleanse and Harmonise Your Clients Aura

Before commencing the Reiki treatment run your hands in your client's aura about six inches above their body from their head right down to their feet in a slow smooth motion at least three times to remove any superficial energy build-ups. This will also bring harmony to your client's aura and form a positive rapport between you and your client. Pay attention to your hands, use your intuition, sense for possible blockages or hot spots to focus on during your healing session. You are now ready to begin the treatment.

Section Eight

Lesson 10: Treating Others with Reiki

Before you begin a full body treatment on another person there are a few important points to remember.
- Never give a Reiki treatment to a person who has a pacemaker as Reiki can alter its rhythm.
- Never give a Reiki treatment to a person who suffers from Diabetes Mellitus and is taking insulin injections, unless they are prepared to check their insulin levels every day as Reiki reduces the amount of insulin they require.

Always explain to a person who is visiting you for the first time for a Reiki treatment exactly what you are going to do and the type of reactions that might occur. Stress that any one of these reactions is normal. They may experience one or two of these reactions, all of them or none of them. It makes no difference. Reiki will go wherever it is needed.

The type of reactions that may occur are:

- A sensation of heat
- A sensation of cold
- See colours
- Past life flashes
- Involuntary movements
- Fall asleep

- Itchiness
- Emotional responses
- Rumbling stomach
- Memory flashes
- Pins and needles
- Sense your hands moving

Often the client will experience extreme cold at the position of your hands while you feel intense heat.
If the client experiences nothing explain to them that the Reiki energy often works on a subtle level yet has profound results which normally become apparent in the following days or weeks.
Never forget the client is drawing Reiki through you. They are doing the healing on a subconscious level. You are only the channel.

Reiki always travels to the place it is needed most.

No knowledge of human anatomy or physiology is required to work with Reiki. Leave your ego aside and Reiki will do the work.

Forget the symptoms treat the whole person.
Listen to your clients' bodies through your hands. Try to sense the different types of energy. If the energy is strong keep your hands

FULL BODY TREATMENT – HAND POSITIONS
Remember the following hand positions are only a guide.

Front Of The Body

First Position: Place your hands over your clients' eyes, wrists just above the forehead. Let your thumbs meet at either side of the nose. Slowly lower your hands and gently touch their face.

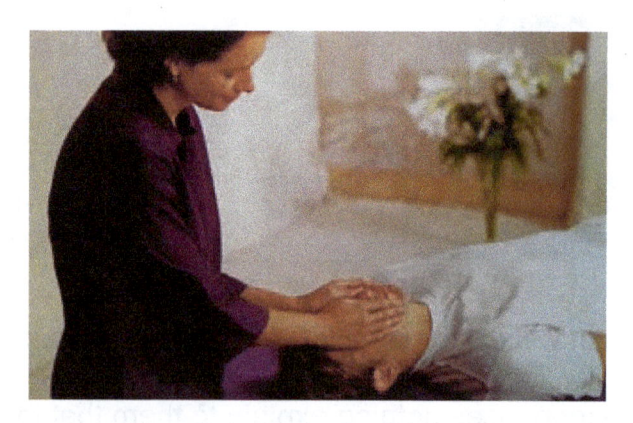

Image: Step-By-Step Reiki (Carmen Fernandez)

Second Position: Gently move your hands up to the temples, fingers resting on the jaw. Remember to not apply pressure onto the temples as this can cause some discomfort for your client.

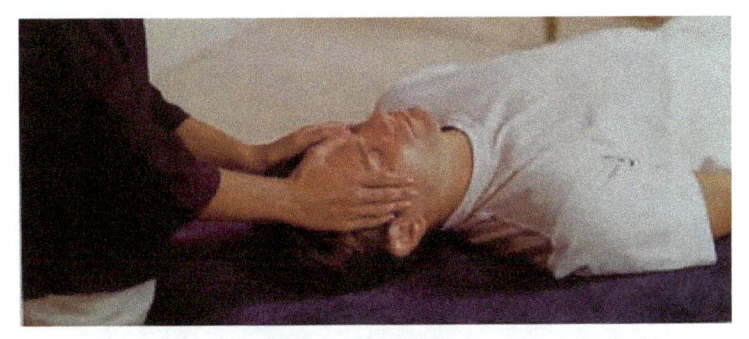

Image: Step-By-Step Reiki (Carmen Fernandez)

Third Position: Gently slide your left hand over the ear to rest under their neck, and with your other hand, gently roll their head onto your flattened hand. Now move your other hand into the same position on the other side of their neck and cup their head gently in both of your hands. Your client will become instantly more relaxed at this point as they rest their head in your hands.

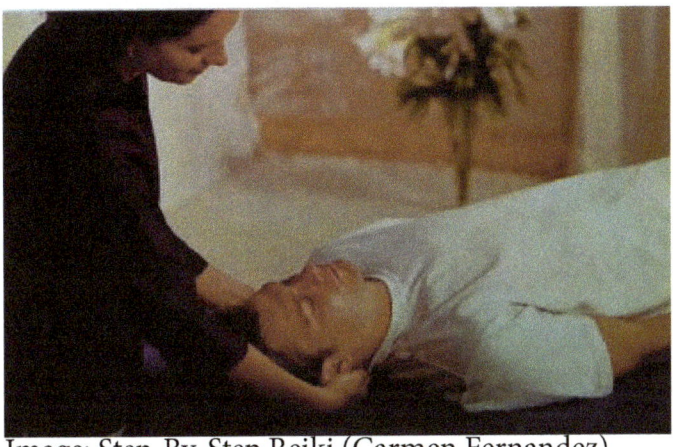

Image: Step-By-Step Reiki (Carmen Fernandez)

Fourth Position: With your left hand, gently roll the clients head onto your right hand. Move your left hand to the bottom of the jaw and throat. Slowly slide your right hand to the same position now. Remember do not rest your elbows on the client at all as this will cause them discomfort. (Fifth Chakra

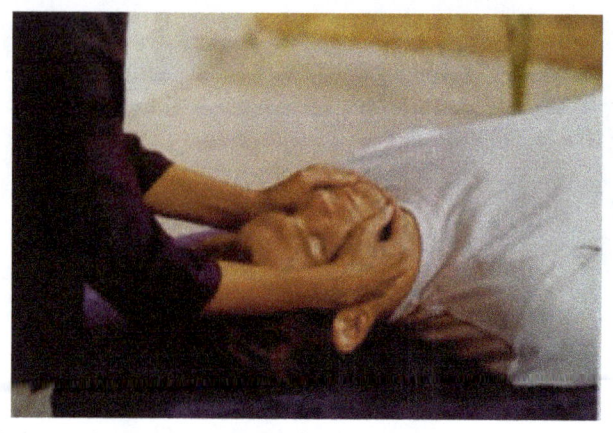

Image: Step-By-Step Reiki (Carmen Fernandez)

Fifth Position: Slide your hands down to rest on the chest, holding them there for a second or two. Gently slide both hands towards the arm, stopping as you reach the armpits. Rest them there for a moment. This allows the Reiki energy to flow into the lymph area. This is great for releasing toxins in the body and also aids in treating the lungs and opening airways. Its perfect for smokers or asthmatics

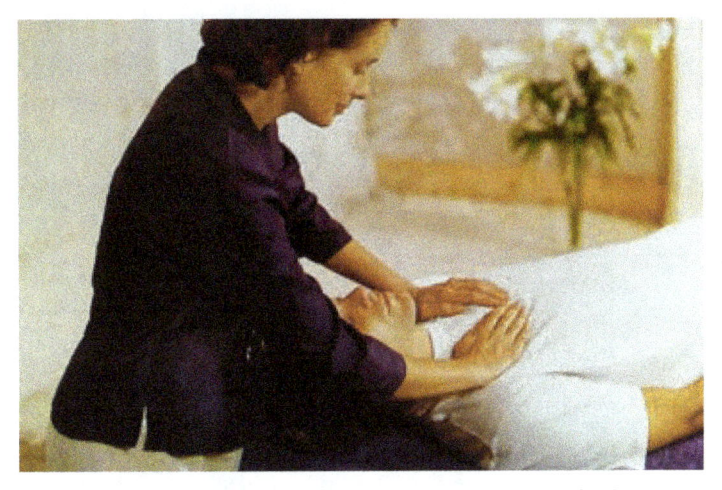

Image: Step-By-Step Reiki (Carmen Fernandez)

Sixth Position: Standing next to your client, place both hands in a straight line across the sternum. This will aid in self-love and love for others. You can hold your hands here for about four minutes or

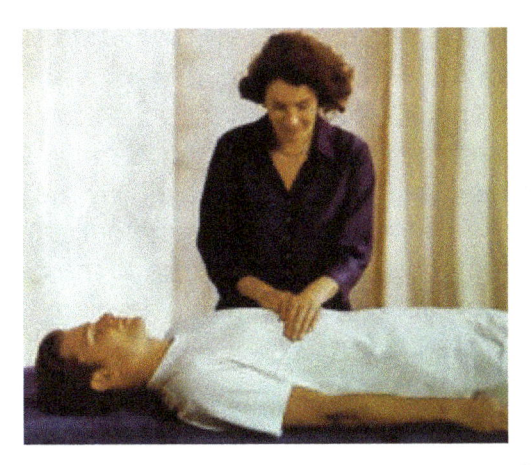

Image: Step-By-Step Reiki (Carmen Fernandez)

Seventh Position: Keep your hands aligned one in front of the other as you give Reiki to the heart chakra, and slowly move them downwards.

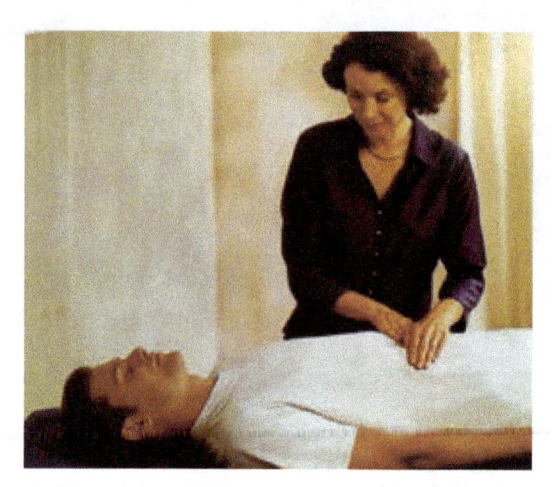

Image: Step-By-Step Reiki (Carmen Fernandez)

Eighth Position: Move your hands to rest over the solar plexus. (Third Chakra). This is where emotions are stored. Your client may experience some emotions here and may even start to cry or feel happy, this is normal. Continue to slowly move down until just above the pelvis (Second Chakra). Rest your hand here for a few minutes. Now move both hands back up to the centre of the chest and hold them here for a few moments, ending the treatment for

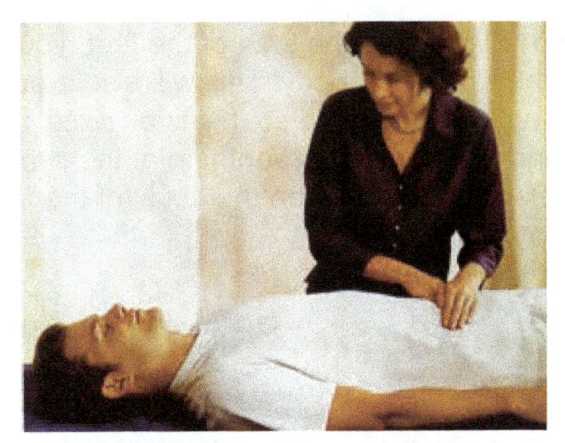

Image: Step-By-Step Reiki (Carmen Fernandez)

Ninth Position: You can now move on to treating the legs as you wish and as often as time allows for. There is no specific way of doing this and I always work on areas I feel may need the additional attention here

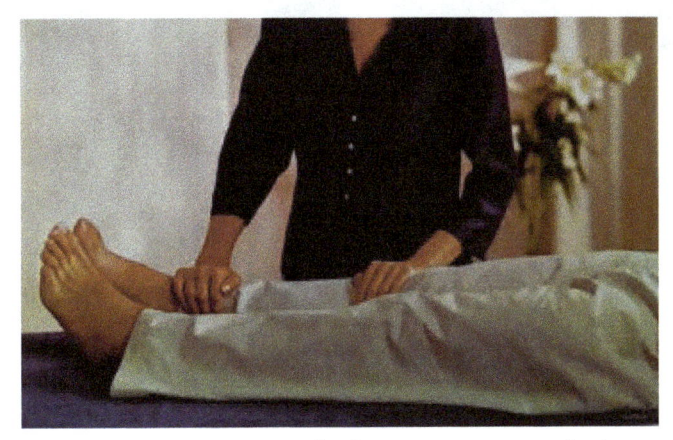

Image: Step-By-Step Reiki (Carmen Fernandez)

Tenth Position: By treating the tops of the feet, you are bringing awareness to the rest of the body. This will also ground the client. They may feel a bit light headed so this is an excellent way to ground them and also feels very soothing at the same time. You can now also place your hands on the souls of the feet as this will awaken a sleepy client.

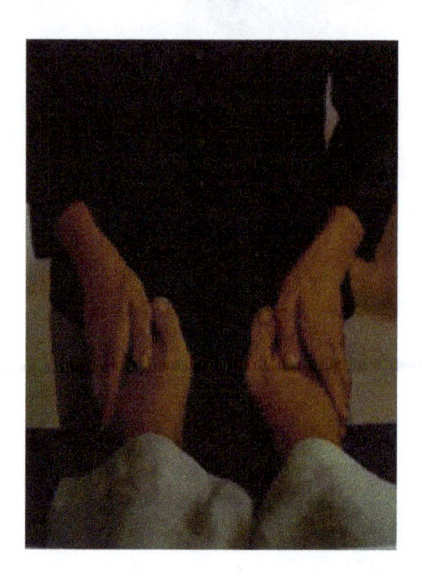

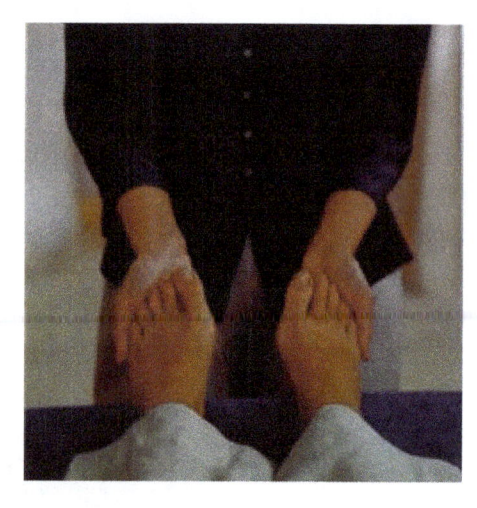

Image: Step-By-Step Reiki (Carmen Fernandez)

To get a better understanding of each Chakra, see the Chakra Healing section of this training manual.

Back of the Body

First Position: When your client has turned over, place your hands on each shoulder, moulding them to their shape. This is not only soothing but also indicates the start of the treatment

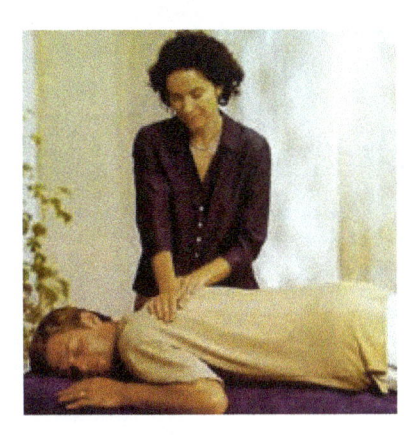

Image: Step-By-Step Reiki (Carmen Fernandez)

Second Position: You can now move your hands down slowly, toward the heart chakra. Rest them here for a moment. This feels especially soothing to your client.

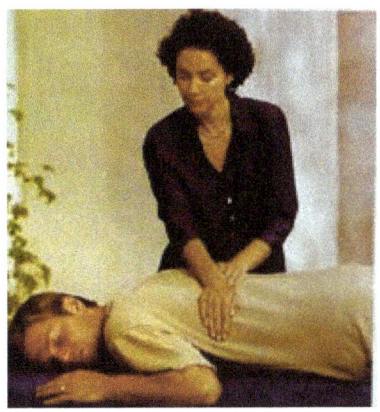

Image: Step-By-Step Reiki (Carmen Fernandez)

Third Position: Move your hands outward so that they are on either side of the clients solar plexus. You can keep slowly moving down toward the kidneys, and the adrenal glands.

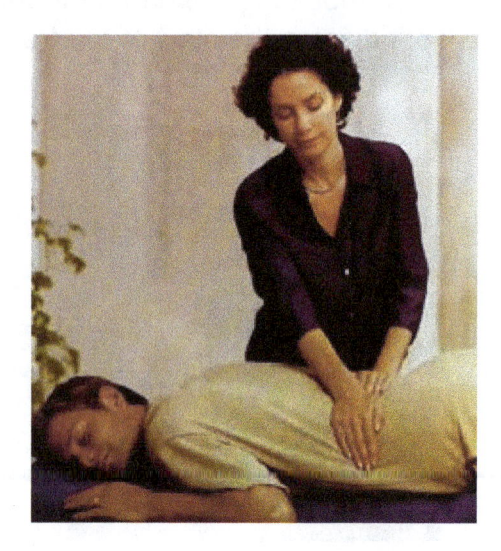

Image: Step-By-Step Reiki (Carmen Fernandez)

Fourth Position: Cup both hands in this area and after a few minutes, slide one hand back up the spine to the base of the neck. Remember to not apply any pressure as this can cause discomfort to your client. This also signals the end of the treatment and also helps to connect the top and base of the back together again energetically speaking.

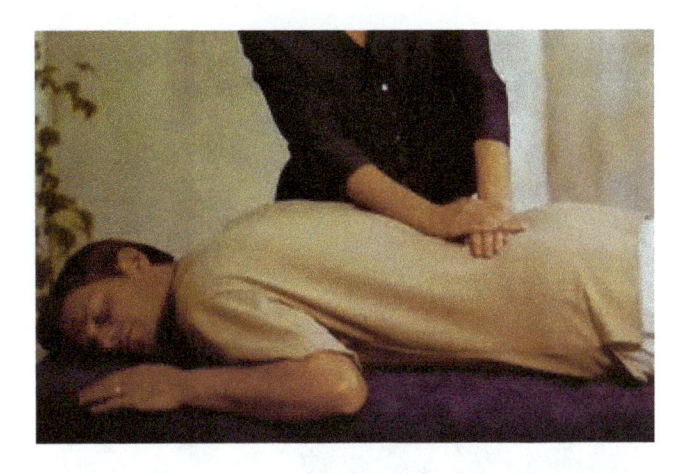

Image: Step-By-Step Reiki (Carmen Fernandez)

Fifth Position: You Can focus on any point on the legs for as long as time allows.

Image: Step-By-Step Reiki (Carmen Fernandez)

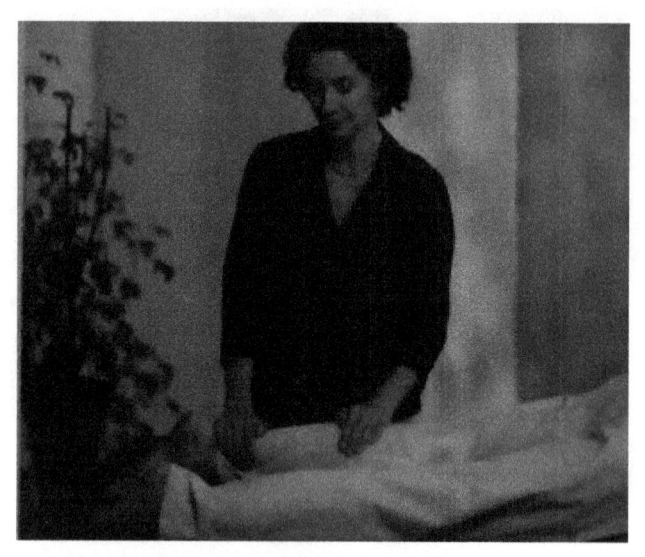

Image: Step-By-Step Reiki (Carmen Fernandez)

Once you have completed the full Reiki treatment its time to end off the session. Move to their feet and kneel down to make the sole eye level. Pressing gently, visualize the Reiki healing/emotional/mental symbol. Now visualize the power symbol on the backs of your hands. You can at this point visualize the distant healing symbol to allow for further healing for up to an hour after their session. You will learn this symbol in Reiki Master Level

Section Nine

Lesson 11: Rapid Reiki Treatment

Rapid Reiki can be performed when you just don't have time for a full session but are in need of a bit of a boost. The following is from an insert and explains how to perform this type of session.

The Rapid Reiki Treatment

Position 1
- 1st Position: (Your client should be seated) Stand behind your client. Place your hands on your client's shoulders.
- Silently make your own personal invocation.

Position 2
- Remain behind your client. Place both hands on the top of your clients head covering the crown chakra.

Position 3
- Move to the side of your client. Place one hand on their forehead at the third eye chakra and the other hand over the occipital ridge at the back of their head.

Position 4
- Remain at the side of your client. Place one hand over the throat chakra at the centre of your clients neck and the other hand parallel on the back of their neck.

Position 5
- Remain at the side of your client. Place one hand on their heart chakra at the centre of their chest and the other hand parallel between your clients shoulder blades.

Position 6
- Remain at the side of your client. Place one hand on the solar plexus and the other hand parallel on the clients spine.

Position 7
- Remain at the side of your client. Place one hand on the base of your clients stomach covering the sacral chakra and the other hand parallel on the base of your clients spine.

Position 8
- Move round to the front of your client and place one hand on each knee.

Position 9
- Kneel down in front of your client and place one hand over each of your clients feet with thumbs open, cupping feet to floor.

Lesson 12: Reiki and Pregnancy, Babies & Children
Pregnancy

Reiki is both safe and extremely beneficial to an unborn child and their pregnant mother. We have found that women who have studied the first degree and are attuned to the universal life force find the experience of pregnancy and childbirth more enjoyable and easier to cope with. Reiki can help during pregnancy in various ways such as:

- Reiki can be used to treat painful muscles, joints, or the spine.
- Reiki strengthens the bond between a mother and her baby. When a mother who is attuned to Reiki places her hands on her tummy she is passing pure unconditional love and healing to her unborn child.

- Reiki keeps the mind-body and spirit in balance reducing the chances of postnatal depression.
- Reiki nourishes the foetus with love and the universal life force. It gently comforts, protects, and envelops the unborn baby.

- ☐ If the father of an unborn baby is a Reiki practitioner he can also help during the pregnancy by treating his partner. The important bond between father and child will also be stimulated each time he places his hands on his partners' pregnant tummy. The father can communicate through his hands with his child.
- ☐ Reiki can help couples who are finding it difficult to conceive a child by reducing stress and stimulating both the females' natural reproductive cycle and the males' production of sperm. In many cases when a couple is desperate for a child they place extreme stress on themselves causing an imbalance of their mind body and spirits.

So often the moment they give up and forget about trying to have children, and the pressure and stress factor is removed many couples find their prayers are answered and pregnancy is discovered.

- ☐ Reiki can accelerate the recovery time of the mother and baby after the birth. It is especially good for caesareans sections and healing the various scars and stitches often associated with childbirth.
- ☐ Reiki can be used to heal the babies' umbilical cord.
- ☐ Reiki can be used to vitalized and nourish the mother's milk if the baby is breastfed. Alternatively, if the baby is to be bottled feed the formula can be treated with Reiki. Treating and enriching the baby's food can help nourish and satisfy the baby's hunger. This will help them suckle until they are content and full. Regular filling feeds lead to fewer sleepless nights. Something all parents pray for.
- ☐ Reiki stimulates balance in the newborn baby. It can easily be channeled to the baby whenever the mother or father (depending on who has been attuned to the energy) touches their child.

Important Note: Always consult your doctor no matter how trivial it may seem if you are concerned about your baby.

Children

- Reiki can be used to treat your children throughout their lives. From the early days and months through puberty, adolescence, and into adulthood.
- Reiki is really great for all their aches and pains. As mentioned at the beginning of this course, we instinctively touch or kiss our children better when they fall or injure themselves. With Reiki, we speed up the healing process and boost their natural healing abilities.
- Use Reiki at bedtime to help your children drift off to sleep.
- Reiki balances your child's mind body and spirit leading to a clearer more focussed approach to life at school and home.
- When a child has an accident they often cry because of the shock. Treat your child by placing one of your hands on their solar plexus and the other at the base of the spine.

Lesson 13: Use Your Imagination

Reiki is present in all living things. Your imagination is the only thing that can set limitations on its uses.
We have listed some of the most common in this lesson.

Reiki and Animals

All animals adore Reiki. Large or small, fierce or friendly. Animals are extremely sensitive to the healing energy of Reiki. Start practicing with your pets and as you become more confident you can move onto other people's pets and animals. As with treating humans Reiki will go where it is needed most. The only difference with animals is that they often guide you to the exact place that requires treatment by moving around until your hand lands on the exact spot. Animals will also let you know when they have had enough by moving away.

There is a huge market for treating animals. Use your imagination to develop your techniques for treatment and develop a marketing strategy. Talk to your local vet or animal welfare center. Advertise; you'll be surprised at the number of people with pets who need and want your help.

Basic Techniques for Animals:

☐ Larger animals such as cats, dogs, horses, and cows normally prefer you to begin by placing your hands behind their ears and working around the body as with a normal full treatment for humans. However, if the animal has a specific injury; place your hands directly over the injury.
☐ Animals that are wild or dangerous can be treated safely through distance healing (second degree).
☐ Another safe way to treat animals is by treating their food and drink. However, this is a weaker form of treatment.

Remember though it is always important to establish trust between you and the animal you are performing Reiki on. We will cover this in more detail in Animal Reiki Course to follow soon.

A Final Thought

By starting with Level 1 Reiki, you have started on an adventure that will lead you on a journey of healing, and growth for both you and your clients. Remember to complete the test at the end of this course and submit it so that you can receive your certificate in Reiki 1. I look forward to seeing you again in Reiki Level II soon. Until then, Happy Healing.

Section Ten
Log Sheet

Name	Contact Number	Treatment	Comments	Signature

Above is your Log Sheet. It is a requirement that you practise on at least 10 people before submitting. You may submit more as the more you practice the better you will become as a Reiki Practioner. This can only be done once you have submitted the test and received your Attunement to Reiki Energy, which can only be done by a Reiki Master.
All tests and Log Sheets can be submitted to info@mysticspirit.co.za for assessment.

Client Consultation Sheet

Confidential Client Case History and Intake Form

Name:

Date:
Address: Phone:
Postal Code: Email:
Date of Birth: Referred by:
Would you like to receive updates via email?

Primary Concerns: Level: 1(hardly notice symptoms) to 10 (symptoms are unbearable)

Medications/Remedies/Supplements & Reason for taking:

Significant Accidents/Injuries:

Please place an X beside any conditions that apply (past or present):

Cancer	Varicose Veins	Allergies:
Heart Disease	H/L Blood Pressure	Surgery:
Diabetes	Paralysis	Genetic Disorders:
Stroke	TMJ Dysfunction	Phobias:
Epilepsy	Arthritis	

Place an X beside any symptoms that you experience:

Headache
Faintness/Dizziness
Tightness in Jaw
Weak body parts
Smoking (#/day___)
Nervousness
Poor Appetite
Excessive Urination
Grinding of Teeth   Heavy feeling in limbs
Blurriness of vision
Constipation
Loose Bowel Movements
Irritated Bowel
Pains in heart/chest
Indigestion
Insomnia
Cold in hands and feet
Lower Back pain
Shoulder/neck pain
Carpel tunnel syndrome
Menstrual Irregularities
Other:

Place an X beside any areas below that you would like improvement in:

Negative self-talk, self-sabotage
Belief in ability to achieve goals
Ability to relax
Ability to use dreams as mental tool for problem solving
Eliminate procrastination
Ability to reach ideal weight
Personal magnetism
Strengthen memory/concentration
Breaking old habits
Release negative events
Ability to align body/mind for self-healing
Ability to take action
Increase learning ability
Beneficial, relationships
Prosperity (attract what you choose)
Attitude and skills at work
Self-Esteem
Youthful Vitality

Below, please describe what you would like to accomplish with these treatments?

Signature: Date:

Consent Form

I,¬_____ (print name) consent to treatment for myself (or my minor child) (print name), and understand that the services provided by the practitioner _____is intended to enhance relaxation and increase communication within my body.

I understand that these services are not a substitute for medical treatment or medications. I am aware that diagnosis is not given and medication is not prescribed. I agree to continue to have regular medical check-ups as part of my overall health care plan.
I understand that participation is voluntary and that at all times I may choose to end my participation. I understand that I may experience 'healing reactions' during the 24 to 48 hours following the services provided.

I understand that any information exchanged during any session is educational in nature and is to be used at my own discretion. I also understand that any information imparted during these sessions is strictly confidential in nature and will not be shared with anyone without my written permission. I do, however, give the practitioner consent to use my case history and results without using my name. I understand that only the practitioner ____ will have access to information in my file to enhance my healing.

I understand that by providing this informed consent I am assuming full responsibility for my services and I hold harmless both the practitioner _____and the facility/location where the services are provided.

I agree to the terms and conditions set out by this consent form and certify that the above information is true and correct. I agree to pay for distance sessions, should I request them.

Signature:_____

Section Eleven

- With your finger, two fingers or all your fingers to draw them in the air in front of you
- Use your palm to draw the symbols on each of your hands
- Draw or visualize the complete symbol in your head
- Appearing in front of you
- Or draw or visualize the symbol over a certain part of the body

How you activate each symbol is not so important. Because it's simply your intention to activate it that starts the flow of energy associated with that symbol.

Level 1 Reiki Symbol

In Usui Reiki there is one Reiki symbol shared with students which is known as the Choku Rei symbol. To draw this symbol, simply begin at the top left and with one continuous stroke, draw the top

Remember to say this Reiki symbols mantra three times as you draw it, chanting Choku Rei, Choku Rei, Choku Rei.

The Cho Ku Rei is a power symbol and works the way a light switch would. By tracing this symbol to the back of your hand or in any of the above mentioned ways, you "switch on" the Reiki Energy. After this you can use any of the other symbols which all have their own form of healing. You will find these symbols in Reiki II and Reiki III. Once you have completed the session you would simply trace this symbol again and thereby "switching off" the Reiki Energy. This however does not stop the energy from working. Reiki Energy will flow to the areas it is most needed and continue to work, even after your client has left.

Reiki I Question Paper

1. True or False

1. Reiki, pronounced Ray-Key, can be translated to mean universal life force
2. The most common misconception is that the Reiki practitioner is your healer when in reality, it is your client who is opening their heart to healing themselves
3. By practicing the discipline of Reiki, you regain your natural ability to heal yourself and others as well as the knowledge you need to lead a happier and more fulfilling life
4. Reiki is a form of electrical healing, originating in India and the East, dating back thousands of years before the time of Christ and Buddha

(4)

2. Name the seven chakras in order

(A) Heart
(B) Throat
(C) Sacral
(D) Solar Plexus
(E) Third Eye
(F) Root
(G) Crown

(7)

3. Where is each Chakra situated?

(7)

4. List the five Reiki Principals:

(5)

5. Write a brief description explaining the initiation ceremony

(5)

6. Which four things should you avoid before the ceremony?

(4)

7. What five symptoms are common after a ceremony?

(5)

8. Name five ways to use Reiki after an attunement

(5)

9. What is the Endocrine System?

(2)

10. Why are hormones important?

(3)

11. Fill in the missing words

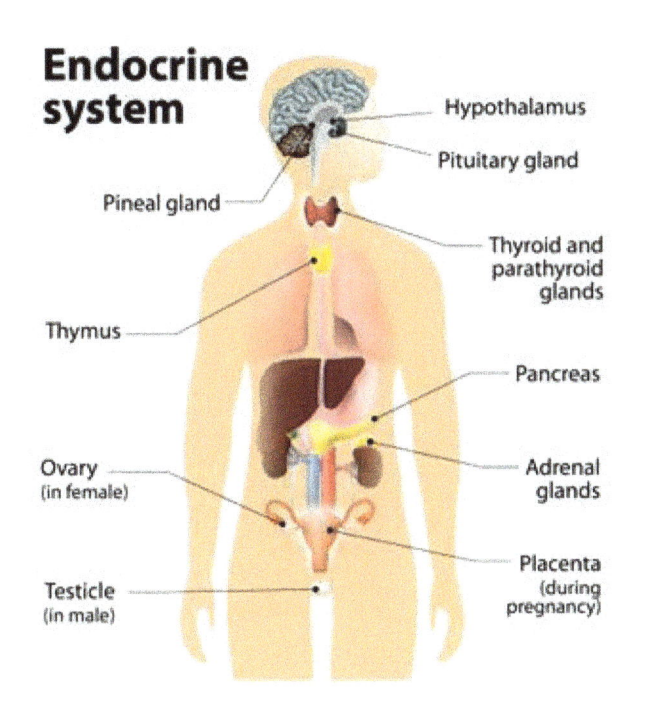

Endocrine system

- Hypothalamus
- Pituitary gland
- Pineal gland
- Thyroid and parathyroid glands
- Thymus
- Pancreas
- Ovary (in female)
- Adrenal glands
- Testicle (in male)
- Placenta (during pregnancy)

(5)

12. What is the Lymphatic System
                                                                                (5)
13. Explain how Reiki unblocks the chakras
                                                                                (10)
14. When may you officially perform Reiki?
                                                                                (1)
15. Name two contraindications to Reiki
                                                                                (2)
16. Is Reiki safe during pregnancy? Support your answer
                                                                                (4)
17. Why is it important to have your client fill in a consultation form?   (2)
18. List four reactions that may occur during a Reiki Session
                                                                                (4)

                                                            Total: (80)